THE COMFORT BAKE

The Comfort Bake

Food that warms the heart

SALLY WISE

murdoch books

Sydney | London

Contents

Introduction

To anyone who knows me, or even just comes to visit, it's very evident that I adore baking – there are nine ovens in total on our small five-acre property here in the Derwent Valley in Tasmania, a region brimming with a diverse range of fresh produce. When we first viewed the property, I was drawn to a small building adjacent to the main house: all I could picture was the opportunity to live out a lifelong dream – to set up a small cooking school, a space where I could bake to my heart's content and share the sheer pleasure of that experience with others.

What makes me so attracted to baking? Perhaps it's because it runs in the family; my great grandparents operated a bakery in Hobart. I never saw it of course – it was way before my time – but even before I came across this piece of family history, I had an innate and undeniable compulsion for baking. Arguably, it's in the blood. There is something about it that just feels right and comfortable.

I've come to realise through the decades that baking is multifaceted in many positive ways. It is in essence an act for yourself, sparking and enabling creativity, but its great strength is that it's something that can be shared readily with others.

One of my grandmothers was inspirational in this respect. She had three corner shelves in her kitchen, stacked with tins of freshly baked treats to serve with a cuppa to anyone who called in, whether it be family, friends, neighbours or even tradespeople. No one ever went away hungry or empty-handed – she always gave them something to take with them for later on.

When I was young I couldn't wait to get my very own kitchen and when our six children came along, what times we had baking together! I am never content unless I have at least 6 metres (20 ft) of bench space, and they would line up along it, some of them on stools or in a high chair. I never bothered with making playdough as other mothers customarily did. Instead we played with all sorts of dough, cake and biscuit mixtures and pastry. Bread was endlessly interesting – the smell, the tactile experience of handling the dough, watching how it performed as it rose, the addition of other supplementary ingredients, the comforting aroma of it baking – a heady combination.

Two grandparents lived with us for many years, so there were always taste-testers ready at hand. A steady stream of friends, neighbours and family called in regularly, so there was plenty of opportunity to share the goodies around.

To fuel the baking, we became very enthusiastic about preserving all manner of seasonal produce. This ensured we had a 'toolbox' of wonderful ingredients in the pantry to make dishes all the more special.

Each summer and autumn people would bring us buckets and boxes of their excess produce. It had no time to spoil: into the preserver, jam jars, sauce or cordial bottles it went. It was a task made light by sharing the workload among us, and the rewards were clear to see and ample for sharing. They were golden years of invention and experimentation, brainstorming, productivity and, most of all, fun with baking.

As is the way of things, the children grew up and left home, and the dynamic changed. However, my husband, Robert, and I surely didn't lose the enthusiasm for seeking out good produce, and I never lost one iota of my love for baking, of which preserving had by now become an integral part.

This passion for preserving somehow came to the ears of ABC Radio Hobart; they were looking to trial a *Jams and Preserves* talkback segment about once a month. That was a decade and a half ago now. At that time the audience was older but that has since changed significantly. Nowadays more and more young people are tremendously interested in knowing where their food comes from, what is in it and how it can be put to best use. The segment soon came to cover a great deal more than the initial topic of jams and preserves, much of it relating to baking. It's been very much a two-way conversation and I have learned so much from listeners who ring or text in with questions, tips and their own family recipes.

For all this baking passion, I have to admit I've never been a fussy cook – I just use basic equipment and easily accessible ingredients. I had my share of failures at the start when I meticulously followed other people's recipes. I just didn't seem to have the knack. I was determined to succeed, however, and so finally came to developing my own.

As my home responsibilities lessened I began teaching in community centres, and very soon realised how beneficial no-fuss, no-fail cooking can be – empowering even. Along with creativity comes a sense of control over the process and resulting end product. I found other people enjoyed it as much as I did. It also promotes self-confidence and contributes to better nutrition. Baking together is a catalyst for communication between generations and cultures at all levels of society and has huge social benefits.

From my perspective, the greatest thing about baking is the capacity to brighten someone's day. The fact that you have thought of them and want to share something you have baked is like offering a 'cuddle with food' – it's warm, it's comforting and asks for nothing in return.

My development of recipes has gone on for decades now, resulting in 15 cookbooks (which include two compilations). I've come to be known as the 'flavour chaser'.

No fancy, special or expensive equipment is necessary to prepare the recipes in this book. You will need a set of scales, a mixing bowl or two, wooden spoons, a whisk, an electric mixer (but it needn't be an expensive stand mixer – hand-held beaters will suffice), a grater and the usual knives, forks, spoons and chopping boards. Keep an eye out at thrift stores for baking trays – I do, and what elation I feel when something is discovered for a mere few dollars (or less). Excellent mixing bowls and other gems can be found there too. It's one of my favourite pastimes; it is recycling and re-homing at its very best – to own a kitchen tool that has been used and loved in someone else's baking experience is really special.

When it comes to ingredients, I have developed certain preferences over the years, which still stand me in good stead. For instance, I always use salted butter in sweet dishes for the sake of consistency, removing the need to add a pinch of salt (after all, everyone's pinch of salt is slightly – sometimes alarmingly – different). In savoury recipes, the salted butter serves to enhance the flavours. I don't generally bother with caster (superfine) sugar as the result is invariably the same as with regular, white (granulated) sugar. Custard

Cooking times will vary depending on your oven. All the recipes in this book were tested in a fan-forced oven; if using a conventional oven, set the temperature 20°C (70°F) higher than indicated in the recipe.

powder is a pantry staple for me as it is convenient, gives excellent results every time without the guesswork, and adds colour and flavour. I prefer maize cornflour (cornstarch) as it performs better than the wheaten equivalent. Usually I don't sift flour, but will generally do so if using it with cocoa, bicarbonate of soda (baking soda) or ground spices, as they can be lumpy at times. Pure icing (confectioners') sugar will almost always need sifting, but if you use the icing sugar mixture as I do (which contains some form of starch), it is often not necessary. The eggs used throughout this book are 65–70 g (2¼–2½ oz) extra large free range.

Actual weights and liquid measurements are used in this book instead of cup measures. This is because cup volume capacity can vary and this inconsistency can cause detrimental end results. All that is needed is a set of digital scales (that need not be expensive) and a measuring jug.

The period of isolation during COVID-19 provided the opportunity for me to dedicate myself to recipe developing. It was a way to pass the time and indulge my passion for baking with the ingredients from my overflowing pantry. (I was very thankful for all the preserving we'd done the previous summer.) Hence this book is different to my others.

After all these years of baking and sharing it about willy-nilly, I've come to be known by many as 'Tasmania's favourite nan'. What a privilege if indeed this were so, to be representative of a whole group in society that has so much they would love to share with the younger generations.

Over the years I've taught cooking classes in various settings: from schools, disability services, community housing and vocational education to under-privileged groups, multicultural groups, university students and even soon-to-be-released female prison inmates. Each of these experiences has been a joy. Without fail I have learned much from innumerable people about both baking and life along the way.

In 2019 I was unexpectedly named Tasmanian Senior Australian of the Year, and in 2021 I was awarded an OAM (Order of Australia Medal) for services to the culinary and hospitality sectors and community. Rather than this being a recommendation for myself, it is about what cooking and baking can offer to each individual, their family and friends and in turn the broader community.

For my part, I will keep on baking into the indefinite future. I know that where we have landed on this little piece of earth is exactly right for us. With the region's abundant and diverse produce and natural beauty, the generosity of our neighbours and larger community, and the capacity to bake for anyone who crosses our path, there is no place I would rather be.

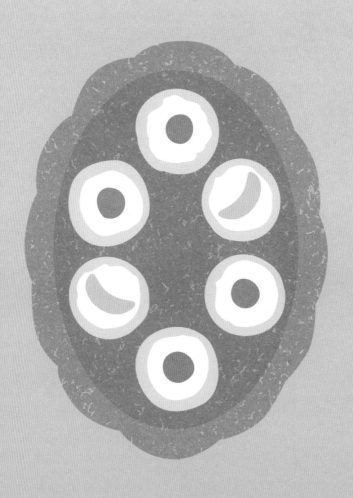

Bite-Sized
Beauties

Summer Cherry or Berry Tarts

MAKES 12

300 g (10½ oz) cherries and/
or seasonal berries such as
strawberries, blackberries,
raspberries or mulberries

FOR THE PASTRY

125 g (4½ oz) very soft
salted butter

125 g (4½ oz) white
(granulated) sugar

1 egg

250 g (9 oz) plain
(all-purpose) flour

FOR THE FILLING

60 g (2¼ oz) sour cream

250 g (9 oz) very soft cream cheese

2 teaspoons finely grated
lemon zest

100 g (3½ oz) icing
(confectioners') sugar,
or to taste

50 ml (1½ fl oz) lemon juice

½ teaspoon vanilla extract

FOR THE GLAZE

100 g (3½ oz) redcurrant
(or other fruit) jelly

These little sweet treats are always a delight. They have a crisp
buttery crust containing a tangy cream filling topped with glazed
cherries or seasonal berries.

~~~~~~~~

To make the pastry

Using a hand whisk, mix the butter and sugar together, then whisk
in the egg until well combined.

Using a large metal spoon, fold in the flour to make a soft dough.
Wrap in plastic wrap and place in the fridge for at least 30 minutes
to firm up before using.

To assemble for baking

Preheat the oven to 190°C (375°F). Grease 12 tartlet tins (preferably
with removable bases).

On a lightly floured surface, roll the dough out to around 6 mm
(¼ inch) thick. Cut into circles to fit the tartlet tins, and press into
place in the tins.

Crumple circles of baking paper (size appropriate) and place in each
tart case. Fill with baking beads or raw rice.

Bake for 10–12 minutes until golden. Remove the paper and baking
beads or rice.

Return the tart cases to the oven and bake for 3 minutes more.

Leave to stand in their tins for 5 minutes before transferring to
a wire rack to cool.

To make the filling

Mix all the ingredients together until smooth.

To prepare the glaze

Heat the redcurrant jelly in a saucepan over low heat on the stovetop
until it is a runny glaze.

To assemble for serving

Spoon the filling into the tarts to two-thirds full.

Top with a selection of cherries and/or berries.

Brush sparingly with the redcurrant jelly glaze and leave to set.

NOTE *Frozen fruit is not suitable for this recipe.*

Vegan Blueberry & Peach Muffins

MAKES 12–15

70 ml (2¼ fl oz) apple purée or
50 g (1¾ oz) finely grated carrot
or 80 ml (2½ fl oz) aquafaba

190 g (6¾ oz) white
(granulated) sugar

grated zest of 1 lemon

juice of 1 lemon or lime

230 g (8½ oz) self-raising flour

190 ml (6½ fl oz) coconut milk

80 ml (2½ fl oz) vegetable oil
or light olive oil

150 g (5½ oz) blueberries,
fresh or frozen

2 peaches, stones removed
and cut into 8 mm (⅜ inch) pieces

The tangy flavours of blueberries and peaches make these simply prepared muffins come to life.

For those choosing to follow a plant-based diet, this recipe is ideal.

~~~~~~~~

Preheat the oven to 180°C (350°F). Line a 15-hole x 50 ml (1½ fl oz) muffin tin with muffin papers to suit.

Whisk together the apple purée, grated carrot or aquafaba with the sugar until well combined.

Add the zest, juice, flour, coconut milk and oil all at once, without stirring, until all are in the bowl. Whisk until the batter is smooth.

Using a large metal spoon, fold in half of the berries and then the prepared peaches.

Spoon evenly into the muffin papers to two-thirds full. Top with the rest of the blueberries.

Bake for 20 minutes, or until golden brown and a metal skewer inserted into the centre comes out clean.

Remove to a wire rack to cool.

Berry & Apple Muffins

MAKES 12–15

2 eggs

190 g (6¾ oz) white
(granulated) sugar

grated zest of 1 lemon

juice of 1 lemon or lime

230 g (8½ oz) self-raising flour

190 ml (6½ fl oz) milk

80 g (2¾ oz) salted butter,
melted

150 g (5½ oz) blueberries,
fresh or frozen

1 large apple, peeled, cored
and finely diced

3 teaspoons icing
(confectioners') sugar,
for dusting (optional)

Virtually any type of berry, fresh or frozen, can be used in this recipe, but strawberries will need to be chopped into smaller chunks.

This is one of my go-to recipes that can be made in a trice when friends or family are coming to call.

Preheat the oven to 180°C (350°F). Line a 15-hole x 50 ml (1½ fl oz) muffin tin with muffin papers to suit.

Whisk together the eggs and sugar in a large bowl until well combined.

Add the zest, juice, flour, milk and butter all at once, without stirring, until all are in the bowl. Whisk until the batter is smooth.

Using a large metal spoon, fold in half of the berries and then the diced apple.

Spoon evenly into the muffin papers to two-thirds full. Top with the rest of the berries.

Bake for 15–20 minutes, or until golden brown and a metal skewer inserted into the centre comes out clean.

Remove to a wire rack to cool.

At serving time, sift a little icing sugar over the top if you like.

Vegan Blueberry & Peach Muffins;
Berry & Apple Muffins
(recipes on pages 16, 17)

*Anzac Biscuits
(recipe on page 20)*

Anzac Biscuits

MAKES 30–36

120 g (4¼ oz) golden syrup

125 g (4½ oz) salted butter, diced

1 teaspoon bicarbonate of soda
(baking soda)

40 ml (1¼ fl oz) boiling water

150 g (5½ oz) plain
(all-purpose) flour

270 g (9½ oz) white
(granulated) sugar

130 g (4½ oz) desiccated coconut

120 g (4¼ oz) rolled oats

1 egg, lightly whisked

½ teaspoon vanilla extract

I've been making these biscuits for almost five decades now. They have always been a particular favourite of my husband, but much debate reigns within our family as to whether they should be chewy or crunchy. With this recipe, it's simply a matter of adjusting the baking time to achieve the desired texture (and you can even make both types to keep everyone happy).

There is always, without fail, a jar of Anzacs on the table for friends who call in. In fact, they have become a firm neighbour-hood favourite.

Preheat the oven to 160°C (315°F). Line four baking trays with baking paper.

Stir the golden syrup and butter together over medium–low heat until the butter is melted and bubbling, then remove from the heat.

In a small bowl, mix together the bicarbonate of soda and boiling water (be aware that this will foam up for a minute or two).

Mix all the dry ingredients together in a large bowl. Make a well in the centre and pour in the golden syrup/butter mixture, the bicarbonate of soda/water mixture, the egg and the vanilla. Stir until well combined.

Leave the mixture to stand for 5–10 minutes to firm up a little.

Roll the mixture into walnut-sized balls and place on the trays, allowing room for them to spread. Press down to flatten just slightly. I find that eight or nine well spaced on a tray is ample.

Working in batches, bake for 10–15 minutes or until golden brown for a chewy biscuit. For a crunchy biscuit, bake a little longer until the biscuits are darker brown.

Allow to cool on the trays for 2 minutes before removing to wire racks to cool completely.

When cool, store in an airtight container. Store the chewy version and the crunchy in separate containers.

NOTE *If the mixture is at first a little sticky, dampen your hands before rolling into balls.*

Very Ginger Gingernuts

MAKES 30–36

125 g (4½ oz) very soft
   salted butter

150 g (5½ oz) white
   (granulated) sugar

40 g (1½ fl oz) golden syrup

1 egg, lightly whisked

200 g (7 oz) self-raising flour

2 teaspoons ground ginger

50 g (1¾ oz) fresh young ginger,
   finely grated

60 g (2¼ oz) crystallised or glacé
   ginger, finely diced

I adore gingernut biscuits and have done so since I was a child. The purchased variety are very nice, of course, but the homemade version is even better.

The incorporation of grated fresh ginger gives these crisp biscuits a vibrant flavour. These biscuits are so popular that they are no sooner baked than they are gone.

~~~~~~~~

Preheat the oven to 170°C (325°F). Line four baking trays with baking paper.

Whisk the butter, sugar and golden syrup together, then whisk in the egg until well incorporated.

In a separate bowl, stir together the flour and ground ginger, then fold into the wet mixture with a large metal spoon.

Finally, fold in the grated ginger (in three lots to ensure even distribution), along with the crystallised or glacé ginger.

Leave the mixture to stand for 5 minutes to firm up a little.

Roll the mixture into walnut-sized balls and place on the trays, allowing room for them to spread. Press down to flatten just slightly. I find that eight or nine well spaced on a tray is ample.

Working in batches, bake for 15–18 minutes, or until the biscuits are golden brown.

Allow to cool on the trays for 2 minutes before removing to wire racks to cool completely.

When cool, store in an airtight container.

NOTE *If the mixture is at first a little sticky, dampen your hands before rolling into balls.*

Mini Chocolate Cream Cakes with Raspberries & Mint

MAKES 12

FOR THE CAKE

3 eggs

250 ml (9 fl oz) milk

290 g (10¼ oz) white (granulated) sugar

40 g (1½ oz) cocoa

1 teaspoon bicarbonate of soda (baking soda)

250 g (9 oz) self-raising flour

180 g (6½ oz) salted butter, melted

20 ml (½ fl oz) apple cider vinegar

FOR THE TOPPING

400 ml (14 fl oz) cream suitable for whipping

2 teaspoons icing (confectioners') sugar (optional)

½ teaspoon vanilla extract

2 teaspoons lemon juice

150 g (5½ oz) raspberry jam

150 g (5½ oz) raspberries

mint leaves, to decorate

These small cakes are welcome anytime. I especially like to make them around Christmas when the colours are very fitting for traditional seasonal fare.

To make the cake

Preheat the oven to 160°C (315°F). Grease a 22 x 30 cm (8½ x 12 inch) slab tin, 6 cm (2½ inches) deep. Line the base with baking paper and grease again.

Using hand-held beaters or a stand mixer, beat the cake ingredients in a bowl for 3 minutes. Transfer to the tin.

Bake for 30 minutes, or until a metal skewer inserted into the centre comes out clean.

Leave to stand in the tin for 5 minutes, before turning out onto a wire rack to cool completely.

To make the topping

Using hand-held beaters or a stand mixer, whip the cream with the icing sugar and vanilla until soft peaks form. Stir in the lemon juice.

To assemble

Cut 6 cm (2½ inch) circles from the cake using scone or biscuit cutters.

Spread each with a teaspoonful of raspberry jam.

Pipe or spoon the cream on top and decorate with the raspberries and mint leaves.

NOTE *The off-cuts from the cake can be frozen and used to make truffles or rum balls at another time.*

Spicy Date & Raisin Rolls

MAKES 18–24

icing (confectioners') sugar,
to serve (optional)

FOR THE PASTRY

200 g (7 oz) plain
(all-purpose) flour

50 g (1¾ oz) self-raising flour

1 teaspoon ground cinnamon

½ teaspoon ground ginger

125 g (4½ oz) cold salted
butter, diced

1 egg yolk, lightly whisked

FOR THE FILLING

220 g (7¾ oz) pitted dates,
roughly chopped

220 g (7¾ oz) raisins

1 teaspoon finely grated
lemon zest

1 teaspoon finely grated
orange zest

60 ml (2 fl oz) lemon juice

90 ml (3 fl oz) orange juice

1 teaspoon ground cinnamon

½ teaspoon mixed spice

These little parcels of goodness are a delicious treat that belie the fact that there is almost no sugar in the mix. The natural sweetness comes from the dates and raisins mixed with spices and citrus. The texture has a pillow-like softness with a gentle crunch from the pastry. These are undoubtedly one of my favourite sweet treats.

~~~~~~~

To make the pastry

Place the dry ingredients and butter in a food processor and process until the mixture resembles breadcrumbs. (Alternatively, this can be achieved by rubbing the ingredients together with your fingers.) Transfer to a bowl.

Make a well in the centre, then pour in the egg yolk and 80–125 ml (2½–4 fl oz) cold water to just bring it together to make a soft dough (don't add more water than is necessary or it will become too wet).

Wrap in plastic wrap and place in the fridge for at least 30 minutes to firm up before using.

To make the filling

Place the filling ingredients and 60 ml (2 fl oz) water in a saucepan and bring to the boil. Reduce the heat to low and simmer for 10 minutes, or until the liquid has been absorbed and the mixture reaches a paste-like consistency. Set aside to cool completely.

To assemble and bake

Preheat the oven to 170°C (325°F). Line two baking trays with baking paper.

On a lightly floured surface, roll the pastry out to a rectangle 30 x 40 cm (12 x 16 inches).

Cut the pastry into three 10 cm (4 inch) wide strips.

Divide the filling into three equal portions and then roll each into a sausage shape and place along the long edge of each strip of pastry.

Dampen the opposite edge of the pastry with a little water and roll up from the filling side to form a log.

Cut each log into eight 5 cm (2 inch) lengths and place on the trays seam side down. Prick each of the rolls with the tip of a sharp knife or a fork.

Bake for 15 minutes, or until golden brown.

Transfer the rolls to wire racks to cool.

If desired, sift a little icing sugar over the top before serving.

Mini Coffee Cakes with Espresso-Infused Icing

MAKES 12

FOR THE CAKES

170 g (6 oz) very soft salted butter

170 g (6 oz) soft brown sugar

3 eggs

180 g (6½ oz) self-raising flour

20 g (¾ oz) instant coffee powder
or granules, dissolved in 20 ml
(½ fl oz) warm water

FOR THE ICING

250 g (9 oz) icing
(confectioners') sugar, sifted

30 g (1 oz) salted butter, melted

25–30 ml (¾–1 fl oz) very strong
espresso coffee

These coffee cakes topped with an espresso-infused icing are perfect for morning or afternoon tea.

To make the cakes

Preheat the oven to 160°C (315°F). Line a 12-hole x 50 ml (1½ fl oz) muffin tin with muffin papers.

Using hand-held beaters or a stand mixer, whisk together the butter and sugar until pale, then whisk in the eggs until creamy. Using a large metal spoon, fold in the flour, then the coffee mixture.

Spoon evenly into the muffin papers.

Bake for 15–20 minutes, or until a metal skewer inserted into the centre comes out clean.

Remove from the tins and cool on a wire rack.

To make the icing

Stir the icing sugar, butter and enough espresso together to make a good spreading consistency.

Spread over the cooled cakes.

Honey Hazelnut Top Cake
(recipe on page 52)

Lamingtons or Jelly Cakes;
Lemong-tons
(recipes on pages 28, 29)

Lamingtons or Jelly Cakes

MAKES 16

FOR THE SPONGE

6 eggs, separated

125 g (4½ oz) white (granulated) sugar

60 ml (2 fl oz) milk

1 teaspoon salted butter

170 g (6 oz) self-raising flour

FOR THE CHOCOLATE COATING

320 g (11¼ oz) icing (confectioners') sugar

20 g (¾ oz) cocoa

2 teaspoons salted butter, melted

boiling water

200 g (7 oz) desiccated coconut

FOR THE RASPBERRY COATING

85 g (3 oz) packet raspberry jelly crystals

280 ml (9½ fl oz) boiling water

3 teaspoons blackcurrant or raspberry cordial syrup (optional)

200 g (7 oz) desiccated coconut

There is debate as to whether the pink jelly coated version actually qualifies as a lamington; many call them jelly cakes. Both are equally delicious, so whatever you choose to call them, a selection of the two makes for prettiness on a platter. For best results, leave the cake overnight before cutting – this helps to prevent it crumbling as it is cut.

To make the sponge

Preheat the oven to 170°C (325°F). Grease a 25 cm (10 inch) square cake tin, 8 cm (3¼ inches) deep and line the base with baking paper. Grease again.

Using hand-held beaters or a stand mixer, whisk the egg whites in a large bowl until thick. Gradually add the sugar and continue beating until stiff glossy peaks form. While still whisking, add the egg yolks one at a time, and beat until thick and creamy.

Meanwhile, heat the milk in a small saucepan over low heat until hot. Stir in the butter to melt, then keep the mixture warm.

Using a large metal spoon, fold the flour into the egg mixture, then gently drizzle the hot milk mixture down the inside of the bowl and fold this in.

Spoon into the tin and gently level out the surface.

Bake for 20–25 minutes, or until well risen and golden and the sponge is starting to pull away from the sides.

Remove from the oven, leave to stand in the tin for 2 minutes, then turn out onto a wire rack to cool completely. Once cooled, store in an airtight container overnight if you have the time – this will make the cake easier to cut. Trim the edges with a serrated knife, then cut into squares or rectangles before coating.

To make chocolate lamingtons

In a heatproof bowl, stir together the icing sugar, cocoa and butter with enough boiling water to make a thin icing. Place the coconut in a bowl. Dip the cake pieces into the chocolate mixture to coat on all sides and then dip in the coconut to coat on all sides. (This is more easily done by using two forks to hold, dip and coat the cake squares.) Place on a wire rack to set.

To make jelly cakes (raspberry lamingtons)

In a heatproof bowl, stir the jelly crystals and boiling water together until the crystals are completely dissolved. Stir in the cordial syrup, if using. Cool, but do not allow to set. Place the coconut in a bowl. Dip the cake pieces into the jelly mixture to coat on all sides and then dip them in the coconut to coat on all sides. (This is more easily done by using two forks to hold, dip and coat the cake squares.) Place them on a wire rack to set.

Lemong-tons

MAKES 12–16

FOR THE CAKE

2 eggs

190 g (6¾ oz) white
   (granulated) sugar

225 g (8 oz) self-raising flour

125 ml (4 fl oz) milk

60 ml (2 fl oz) lemon juice

finely grated zest of 1 lemon

125 g (4½ oz) salted butter,
   melted

FOR THE LEMON COATING

85 g (3 oz) packet lemon
   jelly crystals

375 ml (13 fl oz) boiling water

1 teaspoon finely
   grated lemon zest

200 g (7 oz) desiccated coconut

These are a twist on the old-fashioned lamingtons, but so delicious with the bold flavour of lemon in a buttery cake with a tangy coating. For best results, leave the cake overnight before cutting – this helps to prevent it crumbling as it is cut.

To make the cake

Preheat the oven to 160°C (315°F). Grease a 20 cm (8 inch) square cake tin, 8 cm (3¼ inches) deep and line the base with baking paper. Grease again.

Place all the cake ingredients in a bowl, butter last, and beat using hand-held beaters or a stand mixer for 2 minutes.

Pour the mixture into the tin and gently smooth out the top.

Bake for 25 minutes, or until a metal skewer inserted into the centre comes out clean.

Leave to stand in the tin for 5 minutes before turning out onto a wire rack to cool completely.

Once cooled, store in an airtight container overnight if you have the time – this will make the cake easier to cut. Trim the edges with a serrated knife, then cut into squares or rectangles before coating.

To make the coating

In a heatproof bowl, stir the jelly crystals and boiling water together until the crystals are completely dissolved. Stir in the lemon zest. Cool, but do not allow to set.

Place the coconut in a separate bowl.

Dip the cake pieces into the jelly mixture to coat on all sides and then dip in the coconut to coat on all sides. (This is more easily done by using two forks to hold, dip and coat the cake squares.) Place on a wire rack to set.

NOTE *They are also delicious cut in half and filled with a teaspoonful of Lemon Curd (page 88).*

Orange Butter Bars

MAKES 12–16

These orange-flavoured buttery cake fingers have a tangy orange icing with just a hint of lemon. I am yet to find a person who does not come back for a second serve – they are truly irresistible.

~~~~~~~

FOR THE CAKE

3 eggs

290 g (10¼ oz) white (granulated) sugar

1 tablespoon finely grated orange zest

440 g (15½ oz) self-raising flour

30 g (1 oz) custard powder

125 ml (4 fl oz) milk

90 ml (3 fl oz) orange juice

30 ml (1 fl oz) lemon juice

125 g (4½ oz) salted butter, melted

FOR THE ICING

400 g (14 oz) icing (confectioners') sugar

2 teaspoons salted butter, melted

2 teaspoons finely grated orange zest

60 ml (2 fl oz) orange juice

To make the cake

Preheat the oven to 160°C (315°F). Grease an 18 x 28 cm (7 x 11¼ inch) slab tin, 7 cm (2¾ inches) deep and line the base with baking paper. Grease again.

Using hand-held beaters or a stand mixer, whisk the eggs, sugar and orange zest together until light and fluffy.

Add the remaining cake ingredients (don't stir until all of these are in the bowl) and then whisk together until the batter is smooth.

Pour into the tin and level out. Bake for 30 minutes, or until a metal skewer inserted into the centre comes out clean.

Leave the cake to stand in the tin for 5 minutes before turning out onto a wire rack to cool.

To make the icing

Sift the icing sugar into a bowl and add the melted butter.

Stir in the zest, then gradually stir in enough of the orange juice until a spreadable consistency is reached.

Spread the icing over the cooled cake.

Leave to stand for at least 15 minutes to set before cutting and serving.

Peaches & Cream Butterfly Cakes

MAKES 12

3 teaspoons icing (confectioners') sugar, for dusting

FOR THE FILLING

400 g (14 oz) peaches, tinned or preserved, drained (reserving the juice)

3 teaspoons cornflour (cornstarch) mixed to a paste with 40 ml (1¼ fl oz) cold water

400 ml (14 fl oz) cream suitable for whipping

2 teaspoons icing (confectioners') sugar

3 teaspoons lemon juice

FOR THE CAKES

1 egg

180 g (6½ oz) white (granulated) sugar

3 teaspoons finely grated lemon zest

180 ml (6 fl oz) milk

225 g (8 oz) self-raising flour

60 g (2¼ oz) salted butter, melted

Peaches, lemon and vanilla cream marry together in these delicious little cakes – a tasty twist on the ever popular butterfly cakes.
Make these anytime as a special treat for friends and family.

To make the filling

Cut the peaches into 8 mm (⅜ inch) cubes and place in a saucepan with 100 ml (3½ fl oz) of the drained juice. Bring to the boil and gradually stir in enough cornflour paste to reach a thick custard consistency. Set aside to cool.

Using hand-held beaters or a stand mixer, whip the cream with the icing sugar until firm peaks form, then stir in the lemon juice.

Refrigerate while making the cakes.

To make the cakes

Preheat the oven to 170°C (325°F). Line a 12-hole x 50 ml (1½ fl oz) muffin tin with muffin papers.

Using hand-held beaters or a stand mixer, whisk the egg, sugar and lemon zest together until light and creamy, then all at once, add the milk, flour and melted butter. Whisk until smooth.

Spoon the mixture evenly into the muffin papers to three-quarters full.

Bake for 15 minutes, or until well risen and light golden brown.

Remove from the tin and cool on a wire rack.

To assemble

Cut a slice from the top of each cake and set aside. Place a generous spoonful of the peach mixture on each base, then pipe on a swirl of the cream.

Cut the lids in half and place decoratively on top of the cream.

Dust with the icing sugar.

Spiced Ginger Cookie Sandwiches

MAKES 18–20

FOR THE COOKIES

60 g (2¼ oz) salted butter

220 g (7¾ oz) golden syrup

2 teaspoons finely grated
   lime zest

270 g (9½ oz) plain
   (all-purpose) flour

1 teaspoon bicarbonate of soda
   (baking soda)

2 teaspoons ground ginger

1 teaspoon mixed spice

½ teaspoon ground cinnamon

pinch of ground cloves

3 teaspoons lime juice

FOR THE FILLING

20 g (¾ oz) softened salted butter

60 g (2¼ oz) cream cheese,
   softened

3 teaspoons finely grated lime zest

250 g (9 oz) icing
   (confectioners') sugar

20 ml (½ fl oz) lime juice

These are reminiscent of the flavours of the Caribbean –
a little like a tropical cocktail captured in a soft cookie.

~~~~~~~~~

To make the cookies

Place the butter, golden syrup and lime zest in a saucepan and place over low heat, stirring until the butter is melted. Increase the heat slightly, bring to the boil, then remove from the heat and cool for 15 minutes, stirring occasionally.

Sift the dry ingredients together then, using a large metal spoon, fold into the butter mixture, along with the lime juice.

Leave the dough to stand for 1½ hours (30 minutes will suffice if the mixture is refrigerated, but in this case should be stirred after 15 minutes).

Preheat the oven to 160°C (315°F). Line two baking trays with baking paper.

On a lightly floured surface, roll the dough out to 6 mm (¼ inch) thick.

Cut 5 cm (2 inch) circles from the dough and place on the trays, allowing a little room for spreading.

Re-roll any left-over dough to make more circles. The dough will make 36 to 40 circles, which will be enough for 18 to 20 cookie sandwiches.

Bake for 15 minutes. Remove to a wire rack to cool completely.

To make the filling

Using hand-held beaters or a stand mixer, whisk the butter, cream cheese and lime zest together until smooth, then whisk in the icing sugar, adding enough lime juice to make a good spreading consistency.

To assemble

Place 2 teaspoons of the icing on half of the upturned cookies and then top with the remaining circles. Leave to set.

Rum & Raisin Brownies

MAKES 12–16

FOR THE BROWNIES

120 g (4¼ oz) raisins

90 ml (3 fl oz) rum (any sort)

100 g (3½ oz) dark chocolate, chopped

60 ml (2 fl oz) pouring cream

180 g (6½ oz) softened salted butter

350 g (12 oz) white (granulated) sugar

½ teaspoon vanilla extract

4 eggs

160 g (5¾ oz) plain (all-purpose) flour

¼ teaspoon baking powder

60 g (2¼ oz) cocoa

pinch of sea salt

FOR THE ICING

100 g (3½ oz) dark chocolate, chopped

60 ml (2 fl oz) pouring cream

60 g (2¼ oz) icing (confectioners') sugar, sifted

2 teaspoons rum, or to taste

These delicious brownies, I have to say, are the best I've ever made. The generously rum-soaked raisins give a gourmet quality to this version, which is finished with a decadent rum chocolate fudge icing.

~~~~~~~~

To make the brownies

Soak the raisins in the rum for at least 2 hours.

Preheat the oven to 160°C (315°F). Grease an 18 x 28 cm (7 x 11¼ inch) slab tin, 5 cm (2 inches) deep. Line the base with baking paper and grease again.

Place the chocolate in a small heatproof bowl. Heat the cream to boiling point and then pour it over the chocolate. Cover the bowl and leave to stand for 2 minutes, then stir to melt the chocolate. Set aside and stir every now and then so it does not set.

Using hand-held beaters or a stand mixer, whisk the butter, sugar and vanilla until pale and creamy, then whisk in the eggs until well combined.

In a separate bowl, sift in the flour, baking powder, cocoa and salt. Using a large metal spoon, fold the flour mixture into the butter mixture. Finally, fold in the rum and raisins and the chocolate cream mixture.

Pour the batter into the tin and bake for 30 minutes, or until a metal skewer inserted into the centre comes out clean.

Leave to stand in the tin for 15 minutes, then turn out onto a wire rack to cool.

To make the icing

Place the chocolate in a small heatproof bowl. Heat the cream to boiling point and then pour it over the chocolate. Cover the bowl and leave to stand for 2 minutes, then stir to melt the chocolate. Stir in the icing sugar and rum.

Allow the icing to cool a little until thickened slightly (if necessary) and then spread it over the cooled brownie.

Leave to stand for at least 15 minutes to set before cutting and serving.

Plum Pies

MAKES 24

1 egg white, whisked

FOR THE FILLING

500 g (1 lb 2 oz) plums, weight with stones removed, any variety

60 g (2¼ oz) white (granulated) sugar (quantity will depend on the variety of plum used)

3½ teaspoons cornflour (cornstarch) mixed to a paste with 40 ml (1¼ fl oz) cold water

FOR THE PASTRY

250 g (9 oz) very soft salted butter

250 g (9 oz) white (granulated) sugar

1 egg

440 g (15½ oz) plain (all-purpose) flour

60 g (2¼ oz) custard powder

¼ teaspoon baking powder

These small plum pies are a little unusual in that they can be made from any variety of plum. In fact, even tinned plums could be used in an emergency. However, the best result is achieved when plums are in season, bursting with sunshiny goodness and loads of sweet and sticky juice.

The pastry is laced with a little custard powder for its vanilla tones, which matches very well with the flavour of any plum.

~~~~~~~

To make the filling

Cut the plums into 1 cm (½ inch) pieces and place in a saucepan with 80 ml (2½ fl oz) water. Bring to the boil and then simmer for 5 minutes, stirring often until soft. Stir in the sugar, adding a little more if needed for the sourer varieties. Gradually stir in enough cornflour paste to reach a thick custard consistency. Set aside to cool.

To make the pastry

Using a hand whisk, mix the butter and sugar until pale, then add the egg and whisk again until combined. Using a large metal spoon, fold in the dry ingredients until well combined. Wrap in plastic wrap and place in the fridge for at least 30 minutes to firm up before using.

To assemble for baking

Preheat the oven to 190°C (375°F). Grease a 24-hole x 30 ml (1 fl oz) scoop-shaped patty pan tin.

Cut one-third from the pastry, cover and set aside. Roll the remaining pastry out on a lightly floured surface to around 3 mm (⅛ inch).

Cut 24 x 8 cm (3¼ inch) circles to fit the patty pan tin bases and sides. Press the circles into the holes, then brush with some of the whisked egg white to seal.

Place 2 teaspoons of the plum filling into each pastry case.

Roll out the reserved pastry (re-rolling any scraps from cutting out the bases) and cut slightly smaller circles to cover the tops.

Place the lids over the plum filling, brush with the egg white and crimp the edges with a fork to seal well. Prick each in the centre in a cross shape with the tip of a sharp knife.

Bake for 15 minutes, or until golden brown. Leave the pies to stand in the tin for 5 minutes before removing to a wire rack to cool completely.

NOTE *Any trimmings or left-over pastry can be refrigerated for up to 2 weeks or frozen for 2 months.*

Raspberries & Cream Sponge Fingers

MAKES 12

250 g (9 oz) raspberry jam

300 g (10½ oz) fresh raspberries

3 teaspoons icing
(confectioners') sugar,
for dusting

FOR THE SPONGE

6 eggs, separated

125 g (4½ oz) white
(granulated) sugar

60 ml (2 fl oz) milk

1 teaspoon salted butter

170 g (6 oz) self-raising flour,
sifted

FOR THE FILLING

500 ml (17 fl oz) cream
suitable for whipping

3 teaspoons icing
(confectioners') sugar

½ teaspoon vanilla extract

2 teaspoons lemon juice

A real old-fashioned favourite comes alive with the tang of fresh raspberries and cream, sandwiched between layers of light-as-a-feather sponge fingers.

Any variety of berries with matching jam could be substituted for the raspberries in this recipe.

To make the sponge

Preheat the oven to 190°C (375°F). Grease a 25 cm (10 inch) square cake tin, 7 cm (2¾ inches) deep, and line the base with baking paper. Grease again.

Using hand-held beaters or a stand mixer, whisk the egg whites in a large bowl until thick. Gradually add the sugar and continue whisking until stiff glossy peaks form. While still beating, add the egg yolks one at a time, and beat until thick and creamy.

Meanwhile, heat the milk in a small saucepan over low heat. Stir in the butter to melt, then keep the mixture warm over low heat.

Using a large metal spoon, fold the self-raising flour into the bowl, then gently drizzle the hot milk mixture down the inside of the bowl and fold this in.

Spoon into the tin and gently level out the surface.

Bake for 20–25 minutes, or until well risen and golden and the sponge is starting to pull away from the sides.

Remove from the oven, stand in the tin for 2 minutes, then turn out onto a wire rack to cool completely.

To make the filling

Using hand-held beaters or a stand mixer, whip the cream with the icing sugar and vanilla until a good piping consistency is reached. Stir in the lemon juice.

To assemble

Cut the sponge into 12 fingers. Slice each in half horizontally so that you end up with 24 fingers.

On 12 of the fingers, spread a little of the jam and then pipe on a layer of cream. Place several raspberries along each.

Press another sponge finger on top.

Dust with a little sifted icing sugar.

Bakewell Tarts

MAKES 24

1 egg white, lightly whisked

250 g (9 oz) jam

FOR THE PASTRY

130 g (4½ oz) plain
(all-purpose) flour

30 g (1 oz) almond meal

pinch of baking powder

pinch of sea salt

90 g (3¼ oz) cold salted
butter, diced

1 egg yolk

FOR THE FILLING

125 g (4½ oz) very soft
salted butter

110 g (3¾ oz) white
(granulated) sugar

1 egg

½ teaspoon almond essence

120 g (4¼ oz) almond meal

FOR THE ICING

180 g (6½ oz) icing
(confectioners') sugar

1½ teaspoons softened
salted butter

½ teaspoon vanilla extract

boiling water

12 glacé cherries,
halved (optional)

**FOR THE CREAM AND FRUIT
TOPPING**

250 ml (9 fl oz) cream suitable
for whipping

1 teaspoon icing
(confectioners') sugar

fruit to match the jam in the
tarts (raspberries, apricots,
peaches, strawberries), sliced
if required

These lovely tarts are filled with jam and the flavour of almond,
and traditionally topped with a smear of vanilla icing and half
a glacé cherry. Sometimes I like to top the tarts with whipped cream
and a piece of fresh or preserved fruit to match the jam inside. Any
flavour of jam can be used in these tarts; my favourite is apricot,
but I often use a variety of flavours and prepare some with each.

To make the pastry

Place the dry ingredients and butter in a food processor and pulse until
the mixture resembles breadcrumbs. (Alternatively, this can be achieved
by rubbing the ingredients together with your fingers.) Transfer to a
large bowl.

Whisk together the egg yolk and 50 ml (1½ fl oz) water, then mix this
into the flour mixture to form a soft dough. Wrap in plastic wrap and
place in the fridge for at least 15 minutes to firm up before using.

To make the filling

Using a hand whisk, mix the butter and sugar together until pale,
then mix in the egg until creamy. Use a large metal spoon to fold in
the almond essence and almond meal.

To assemble for baking

Preheat the oven to 160°C (315°F). Grease a 24-hole x 30 ml (1 fl oz)
scoop-shaped patty pan tin.

On a lightly floured surface, roll the pastry out to around 3 mm (⅛ inch)
and cut out 24 x 8 cm (3¼ inch) circles to fit into the tin. Press the circles
into the holes and brush with a little of the whisked egg white to seal.

Place ½ a teaspoon of jam in the base of each. Top each tart with
2 teaspoons of the almond mixture.

Bake for 20 minutes, or until golden brown and set. Allow to stand in
their tin for 5 minutes, then remove to a wire rack to cool completely.

To make the icing

Sift the icing sugar into a bowl, add the butter and vanilla, then stir in
enough boiling water – a little at a time – to make a smooth spreading
consistency. Spread over the cooled tarts and top with half a glacé
cherry (if using).

To make the cream and fruit topping

Using hand-held beaters or a stand mixer, whip the cream with the
icing sugar until soft peaks form. Place a spoonful on each tart and top
with fruit.

Cakes

Coffee Hazelnut Cake with Espresso Drizzle

SERVES 8

FOR THE CAKE

2 eggs

200 g (7 oz) white
(granulated) sugar

125 ml (4 fl oz) milk

180 g (6½ oz) self-raising flour

40 ml (1¼ fl oz) coffee
and chicory essence

90 g (3¼ oz) salted butter, melted

60 g (2¼ oz) hazelnuts,
roughly chopped

FOR THE DRIZZLE

320 g (11¼ oz) icing
(confectioners') sugar

1 teaspoon instant coffee
powder or granules dissolved
in 2 teaspoons hot water

1½ teaspoons coffee
and chicory essence

2 teaspoons salted butter, melted

3 teaspoons hot, strong
espresso coffee,
plus extra if needed

70 g (2½ oz) hazelnuts, chopped

This is coffee cake in the truest sense – not just a treat to serve with a cuppa, but one that enhances the whole coffee experience.

The cake is flavoured with the old-fashioned yet still popular coffee and chicory essence, which does not dry out the cake as other forms of coffee are wont to do. This flavouring is also included in the icing to reinforce the coffee element, but not overpower it. The essence is readily available at supermarkets.

A generous amount of hazelnuts complete the appeal of this delicious cake.

~~~~~~~

To make the cake

Preheat the oven to 160°C (315°F). Liberally grease a 20 cm (8 inch) bundt tin (or ring tin). Dust the tin with a thin layer of flour, then turn it over and tap away any excess flour.

Place all the cake ingredients except the hazelnuts in a large bowl, melted butter last, and beat with hand-held beaters or a stand mixer for 2 minutes. Using a large metal spoon, fold in the hazelnuts.

Pour the mixture evenly into the tin and bake for 30–40 minutes, or until a metal skewer inserted into the cake comes out clean.

Leave to stand in the tin for 5 minutes, then turn out onto a wire rack to cool.

To make the drizzle

With a metal spoon, mix together all the drizzle ingredients except the hazelnuts, adding a little extra espresso (a few drops at a time) until a pouring consistency is reached.

Transfer to a jug and add the chopped hazelnuts, then pour over the cooled cake and serve immediately.

Yoghurt Citrus Cake

SERVES 8

FOR THE CAKE

260 g (9¼ oz) Greek-style
   or natural yoghurt

3 eggs

200 g (7 oz) white
   (granulated) sugar

125 ml (4 fl oz) vegetable
   or light olive oil

30 g (1 oz) honey

150 g (5½ oz) self-raising flour

70 g (2½ oz) plain
   (all-purpose) flour

3 teaspoons finely grated
   lemon zest

2 teaspoons finely grated
   orange zest

2 teaspoons finely grated
   lime zest

20 ml (½ fl oz) lemon juice

20 ml (½ fl oz) orange juice

20 ml (½ fl oz) lime juice

FOR THE GLAZE

20 ml (½ fl oz) lemon juice

20 ml (½ fl oz) orange juice

20 ml (½ fl oz) lime juice

100 g (3½ oz) white
   (granulated) sugar

This cake is bursting with the bold and beautiful flavours of oranges and lemons. The creaminess of yoghurt adds to the sensation of tart and sweet – it's a thoroughly delicious taste experience. The citrus flavours are further emphasised in a tangy glaze that makes the cake glisten.

Coconut yoghurt can be substituted for the Greek-style yoghurt. The cake's texture will just be slightly denser.

To make the cake

Preheat the oven to 160°C (315°F). Grease a 20 cm (8 inch) round cake tin, 6 cm (2½ inches) deep. Line the base with baking paper and grease again.

Whisk together the yoghurt, eggs, sugar, oil and honey until smooth. In a separate bowl, combine the flours, then whisk the flours into the yoghurt mixture, along with the citrus zest and juice, until smooth.

Spoon into the tin.

Bake for 1 hour, or until a metal skewer inserted into the centre comes out clean.

Leave to stand in the tin for 10 minutes while you make the glaze.

To make the glaze

Place the juice and sugar in a saucepan. Bring to the boil, stirring, then reduce the heat and simmer for 5 minutes.

To assemble

Turn the cake out onto a wire rack (and invert it so it's the right way up). Position a plate underneath the rack so that it sits under the cake.

Prick the cake all over with a skewer at 8 mm (⅜ inch) intervals. Spoon the warm glaze over the warm cake – some glaze will inevitably spill over onto the plate below.

Leave the cake until cool or lukewarm, spooning the extra glaze that has spilled onto the plate over the cake from time to time.

Finally, lift the cake onto the plate – the remaining glaze makes the base of the cake supremely delicious.

Chocolate Chestnut Cake

SERVES 8

FOR THE CAKES

3 eggs

250 ml (9 fl oz) milk

290 g (10¼ oz) white (granulated) sugar

1 teaspoon bicarbonate of soda (baking soda)

40 g (1½ oz) cocoa

250 g (9 oz) self-raising flour

180 g (6½ oz) salted butter, melted and cooled slightly

20 ml (½ fl oz) apple cider vinegar

FOR THE CHESTNUT CREAM

435 g (15½ oz) chestnut purée

600 ml (21 fl oz) cream suitable for whipping

2 teaspoons lemon juice

3 teaspoons icing (confectioners') sugar

1 teaspoon vanilla extract

FOR THE CHOCOLATE SHARDS

90 g (3¼ oz) dark chocolate, chopped

This luxurious cake has four layers of chestnut cream and rich chocolate sponge, and is finished with swirls of extra chestnut cream and delicious chocolate shards. It's a cake for special occasions that's very simple to prepare. You may need to visit a delicatessen to obtain the chestnut purée, but it is worth the effort to track it down.

To make the cakes

Preheat the oven to 160°C (315°F). Grease two round 20 cm (8 inch) cake tins, each 8 cm (3¼ inches) deep. Line the bases with baking paper and grease again. Using hand-held beaters or a stand mixer, beat all the cake ingredients together for 3 minutes. Transfer to the tins, ensuring each contains the same amount. Bake for 30 minutes, or until a metal skewer inserted into the centre comes out clean. Leave to stand in the tins for 5 minutes, before turning out onto wire racks to cool completely.

To make the chestnut cream

Place the chestnut purée and 120 ml (4 fl oz) water in a saucepan and heat, whisking to break up the purée, until it is smooth and creamy. Remove from the heat and blend with a stick blender. Leave to cool, stirring now and then so it doesn't harden. Stir in 125 ml (4½ fl oz) of the cream, the lemon juice, icing sugar and vanilla. Using hand-held beaters or a stand mixer, whip the remaining cream to soft peaks and then, working in batches, fold it into the chestnut mixture, one-quarter at a time. Beat until the mixture looks like whipped cream, just firm enough to pipe.

To make the chocolate shards

Put the chocolate into a heatproof bowl and place over a saucepan of barely simmering water (ensure that the base of the bowl does not touch the water). Stir until melted. Alternatively, melt in the microwave on medium in 20-second bursts, stirring after each burst, until the chocolate has melted. Turn out onto a cool surface and leave to barely set – this will only take a few minutes at most. Scrape with a wide metal spatula or cheese slicer to form shards or curls.

To assemble

Cut each of the chocolate cakes in half horizontally with a long serrated knife and place one layer on a serving platter. Top with a quarter of the chestnut cream and spread out to cover. Repeat this process twice more, and then place the final layer of cake on top. Spread a thin layer of the remaining cream on top. With the left-over mixture, transfer to a piping bag fitted with a star nozzle and pipe swirls at intervals around the top of the cake. Decorate with the chocolate shards or curls. Refrigerate for at least 1 hour before cutting into slices to serve.

Pistachio Orange Drizzle Cake

SERVES 6–8

40 g (1½ oz) pistachio kernels, chopped

FOR THE CAKE

3 eggs

200 g (7 oz) white (granulated) sugar

160 g (5¾ oz) self-raising flour

125 ml (4 fl oz) milk

1 tablespoon finely grated orange zest

125 g (4½ oz) salted butter, melted

120 g (4¼ oz) pistachio kernels, roughly chopped

FOR THE DRIZZLE

200 g (7 oz) icing (confectioners') sugar

1 teaspoon finely grated orange zest

1 teaspoon salted butter, melted

40 ml (1¼ fl oz) orange juice

3 teaspoons lemon juice

The delightful crunch of pistachios comes together with orange in this rich butter cake, which is topped with a brightly flavoured orange drizzle for extra tang.

~~~~~~~

To make the cake

Preheat the oven to 160°C (315°F). Grease an 18 cm (7 inch) round cake tin, 7 cm (2¾ inches) deep. Line the base with baking paper and grease again.

Using hand-held beaters or a stand mixer, beat all the cake ingredients except the pistachios for 2 minutes. Fold in the pistachios.

Spoon the cake batter evenly into the tin.

Bake for 50–60 minutes, or until a metal skewer inserted into the centre comes out clean.

Leave to stand in the tin for 5 minutes before turning out onto a wire rack to cool completely.

To make the drizzle

Mix together the icing sugar, orange zest and butter and then stir in the orange juice and enough lemon juice to make a pouring consistency.

Spoon the drizzle over the cooled cake and sprinkle with the pistachios.

Honey Hazelnut Top Cake

FOR THE CAKE

125 g (4½ oz) softened salted butter

100 g (3½ oz) white (granulated) sugar

150 g (5½ oz) honey

2 eggs

300 g (10½ oz) self-raising flour

1 teaspoon bicarbonate of soda (baking soda)

1 teaspoon ground cinnamon

1 teaspoon mixed spice

¼ teaspoon ground cloves

180 ml (6 fl oz) milk

FOR THE HONEY NUT TOPPING

150 g (5½ oz) honey

50 g (1¾ oz) soft brown sugar

60 g (2¼ oz) softened salted butter

90 g (3¼ oz) coarsely chopped hazelnuts

There are few nicer combinations than nuts mixed with honey turned crisp by the process of baking. This spiced butter cake is topped with just such a combination and makes one of the most delicious morning or afternoon tea treats.

~~~~~~~

To make the cake

Preheat the oven to 160°C (315°F). Grease a 20 cm (8 inch) round springform cake tin, 8 cm (3¼ inches) deep.

Using hand-held beaters or a stand mixer, whisk together the butter, sugar and honey until well combined and creamy, then add the eggs and beat until well combined.

In a separate bowl, sift together the flour, bicarbonate of soda and spices then, using a large metal spoon, fold it into the honey mixture in batches, alternating with the milk.

Pour into the tin and bake for 40 minutes, or until a metal skewer inserted into the centre comes out clean.

To make the topping

While the cake is baking, place all the topping ingredients in a saucepan and heat over low heat until well combined. Allow to cool but not set. If this happens, simply reheat for a moment over low heat.

Remove the cake from the oven, spoon the honey nut topping over the cake and return it to the oven for 5 minutes more.

Leave the cake, still in the tin, on a wire rack to cool.

When cool, remove the outer ring and then sit the cake, still on its base plate, on a serving platter.

Sticky Date Surprise Cake

SERVES 8–12

FOR THE CAKE

120 g (4¼ oz) pitted dates, roughly chopped

150 g (5½ oz) raisins

200 g (7 oz) white (granulated) sugar

150 g (5½ oz) zucchini (courgette), coarsely grated

60 ml (2 fl oz) extra virgin olive oil

1 teaspoon bicarbonate of soda (baking soda)

3 teaspoons marmalade (any sort)

3 teaspoons lemon juice

2 eggs, whisked

320 g (11¼ oz) self-raising flour

FOR THE GLAZE

220 g (7¾ oz) soft brown sugar

150 ml (5 fl oz) coconut milk

1 teaspoon vanilla extract

60 g (2¼ oz) salted butter

Summary: Summer here in the Derwent Valley is a sight to behold with the enormous number of zucchini – anyone who has a vegetable garden has plenty to share. Zucchini recipes are always in high demand. So I developed this cake to help deal with the glut . . . nobody has ever been able to spot the zucchini!

To make the cake

Preheat the oven to 170°C (325°F). Grease an 18 x 28 cm (7 x 11¼ inch) slab tin, 7 cm (2¾ inches) deep.

Place the dates, raisins, sugar, grated zucchini, oil, bicarbonate of soda, marmalade, lemon juice and 250 ml (9 fl oz) water in a large saucepan and bring to the boil, stirring to dissolve the sugar. As soon as it has boiled, remove from the heat and leave to cool for 15 minutes.

Add the eggs and self-raising flour and mix well.

Pour into the tin and level out with a spatula.

Bake for 30 minutes, or until a metal skewer inserted into the centre comes out clean.

Leave to stand for a few minutes while you make the glaze.

To make the glaze

Combine the sugar, coconut milk, vanilla and butter in a saucepan. Bring to boiling point, then simmer for 5 minutes.

To assemble

Using a fork, poke holes in the cake at 8 mm (⅜ inch) intervals and drizzle the glaze over.

Wait until serving time to cut into pieces and serve straight from the tin.

Honey Caramel Topsy Turvy Pear Cake

SERVES 8–12

825 g (1 b 13 oz) pear halves,
 drained if tinned

FOR THE HONEY CARAMEL

125 g (4½ oz) salted butter

125 g (4½ oz) soft brown sugar

20 g (¾ oz) honey, plus
 20 g extra, for glazing

FOR THE CAKE

2 eggs

200 g (7 oz) white
 (granulated) sugar

125 ml (4 fl oz) milk

230 g (8½ oz) self-raising flour

finely grated zest of 1 lemon

125 g (4½ oz) salted butter,
 melted and cooled slightly

The autumnal flavour of pears in a rich butter caramel, topped with a drizzle of honey, makes this a most delicious cake.
 Fresh, tinned or preserved pears can be used in this recipe.

Preheat the oven to 160°C (315°F). Grease a 23 x 30 cm (9 x 12 inch) slab tin, 6 cm (2½ inches) deep. Line the base with baking paper and then grease again.

To make the honey caramel

Melt the butter, brown sugar and honey together. Bring to the boil and simmer for 1 minute, whisking.

Pour into the base of the tin.

Cut each pear half into four slices, and place them decoratively over the caramel.

To make the cake

Using hand-held beaters or a stand mixer, beat all the cake ingredients for 2 minutes.

Spoon the batter over the pears, then carefully level the mixture with a spatula, leaving it just slightly concave in the middle.

Bake for 30–40 minutes, or until a metal skewer inserted into the centre comes out clean.

Allow to stand for 5 minutes before turning the cake out onto a wire rack; the pears will be on top. Position a plate underneath the rack so that it sits under the cake. (This way any spilled caramel can be retrieved by spooning it up and over the cake.)

Heat the extra honey in a small saucepan until warmed through and runny, then spoon over the cake.

Cool the cake for 15 minutes before cutting into squares to serve.

Strawberry Shortcake

2 sheets ready-rolled puff pastry, thawed

300 g (10½ oz) strawberries, to decorate

FOR THE CAKE

60 ml (2 fl oz) milk

25 g (1 oz) natural or Greek-style yoghurt

70 ml (2¼ fl oz) light olive oil or vegetable oil

20 ml (½ fl oz) lemon juice

1 teaspoon finely grated lemon zest

2 eggs

120 g (4¼ oz) white (granulated) sugar

225 g (8 oz) self-raising flour

FOR THE FILLING

900 ml (30½ fl oz) cream suitable for whipping

3 teaspoons icing (confectioners') sugar

125 g (4½ oz) soft ricotta

20 g (¾ oz) natural or Greek-style yoghurt

3 teaspoons lemon juice

250 g (9 oz) strawberry jam (or redcurrant jelly)

This cake is one of the prettiest and most delicious cakes of all.

A perfect balance of crisp and creamy is provided by discs of puff pastry enclosing a buttery sponge and is further enhanced by strawberry jam, a spritely ricotta cream and fresh strawberries as its signature finishing flourish. It is without doubt the most popular of all the cakes I bake – a definite crowd-pleaser.

~~~~~~~~

To make the pastry layers

Preheat the oven to 200°C (400°F). Have two baking trays ready, one lined with baking paper.

On a lightly floured surface, roll one of the pastry sheets out to around 28 cm (11¼ inches) square.

Place on the lined tray. Cover with a sheet of baking paper and place the other tray on top.

Bake for 10 minutes, or until the pastry is golden brown. Remove to a wire rack to cool, and then repeat this process with the remaining pastry sheet.

Cut a 23 cm (9 inch) round from each pastry sheet and set aside.

To make the cake

Reduce the oven temperature to 160°C (315°F). Grease a round 23 cm (9 inch) cake tin, 6 cm (2½ inches) deep, and line the base with baking paper. Grease again.

Combine the milk, yoghurt and oil, mixing until smooth. Add the lemon juice and zest and stir until combined. Set aside.

Using hand-held beaters or a stand mixer, whisk the eggs and sugar together until thick and creamy.

A little at a time, add the milk mixture to the egg mixture, alternating with the flour, and stirring until the mixture is smooth.

Spoon into the cake tin and level out.

Bake for 25 minutes, or until a metal skewer inserted into the centre of the cake comes out clean.

Leave to stand in the tin for 5 minutes before turning out onto a wire rack to cool completely.

recipe continued overleaf

Strawberry Shortcake . . . cont'd

To prepare the filling

When you are ready to assemble, use hand-held beaters or a stand mixer to whip the cream with the sugar until soft peaks form. With the motor running, add the ricotta, yoghurt and lemon juice and whisk to a medium–firm consistency.

To assemble

Place a little dab of the cream mixture in the centre of a large serving platter. Place one of the discs of pastry on this, then spread with a quarter of the strawberry jam and a third of the cream mixture.

Trim the top of the cooled cake so it's level, then carefully slice the cake in half horizontally using a serrated knife.

Spread one half with another quarter of the jam and sandwich the other cake layer on top.

Place the sandwiched cake on top of the cream-covered pastry disc. Spread with another quarter of the jam, then another third of the cream mixture and finally top with the remaining disc of pastry.

Spread this with the remaining jam. Top with the final third of the cream mixture. Finish by placing the strawberries around the edge. Refrigerate for at least 1 hour before serving.

German Apple Cake

SERVES 6

60 g (2¼ oz) very soft salted butter, plus 20 g (¾ oz) extra

200 g (7 oz) white (granulated) sugar, plus 1 teaspoon extra

1 egg

150 g (5½ oz) plain (all-purpose) flour

½ teaspoon baking powder

1 teaspoon ground cinnamon, plus ½ teaspoon extra

½ teaspoon ground nutmeg

½ teaspoon ground ginger

¼ teaspoon bicarbonate of soda (baking soda)

300 g (10½ oz) green apples (such as granny smith or golden delicious), peeled, cored and thinly sliced

This is an impressively moist cake and very easy to make. It is filled with the flavour and crunch of apple slices and topped with a buttery cinnamon and sugar crust.

This recipe is adapted from one given to me by an elderly German friend many decades ago. It had been handed down through many generations of her family and was a great favourite.

~~~~~~

Preheat the oven to 160°C (315°F). Grease an 18 cm (7 inch) round cake tin, 7 cm (2¾ inches) deep, and line the base with baking paper. Grease again.

Using hand-held beaters or a stand mixer, whisk together the 60 g (2¼ oz) of butter and the sugar until pale and creamy, and then add the egg and whisk until light and fluffy.

In a separate bowl, use a large metal spoon to combine the flour, baking powder, 1 teaspoon of the cinnamon, the nutmeg, ginger and bicarbonate of soda. Add the dry ingredients to the butter mixture and mix to form a firm batter. Stir the apples slices through. (You may need to use your hands to do this effectively.)

Spoon into the tin and level out with the back of a damp spoon.

Bake for 30 minutes, or until a metal skewer inserted into the centre comes out clean.

Leave to stand in the tin for 5 minutes, then turn out onto a wire rack.

Melt the extra 20 g (¾ oz) of butter, then brush over the warm cake. Combine the extra cinnamon and sugar and sprinkle over the top.

Serve warm or cold.

Plum Crumble Cake

SERVES 6–8

1 egg white, whisked

FOR THE BASE

1 egg

120 g (4¼ oz) white (granulated) sugar

1 teaspoon finely grated lemon zest

160 g (5¾ oz) plain (all-purpose) flour

125 g (4½ oz) self-raising flour

150 g (5½ oz) salted butter, melted and cooled slightly

FOR THE FILLING

500 g (1 lb 2 oz) plums – fresh, tinned or preserved

2 eggs

1 egg yolk

150 ml (5 fl oz) pouring cream

150 g (5½ oz) sour cream

60 g (2¼ oz) white (granulated) sugar

1 teaspoon cornflour (cornstarch)

3 teaspoons lemon juice

This continental-style cake is very easy to make and yet it results in three delicious layers that melt in the mouth, and a contrasting thin film of caramel crumble that forms on top.

It could easily be served as a dessert with custard, crème fraîche or ice cream. However it is exceptional for morning or afternoon tea – a real treat for those with whom you choose to share it.

~~~~~~

Preheat the oven to 180°C (350°F). Grease a 20 cm (8 inch) round springform cake tin, 8 cm (3¼ inches) deep.

To make the base

In a large bowl, whisk together the egg, sugar and lemon zest until thick and creamy. Combine the flours in a separate bowl then, using a metal spoon, fold them into the egg mixture, along with the melted butter, mixing well.

Spoon three-quarters of the mixture into the tin. Press the mixture down into the base and up the side to a depth of 8 mm (⅜ inch). This will contain the filling.

Brush the base with some of the whisked egg white to seal.

To make the filling

Halve the plums and remove the stones. Place them on paper towel to soak up any excess liquid, then arrange on top of the base cut side up.

Whisk together the eggs, egg yolk, cream, sour cream, sugar, cornflour and lemon juice until well combined. Carefully pour this liquid over the fruit.

To assemble for baking

Spoon the last of the base mixture evenly over the top.

Bake for 10 minutes, then reduce the oven temperature to 160°C (315°F) and bake for 20–25 minutes more, or until the topping is set.

Leave to stand for 15 minutes before releasing the side of the tin and cutting into slices to serve.

NOTE I like to use greengage plums (which I preserve in the summer); however, tinned or other fresh plum varieties could be substituted. Other fruit could also be used – in autumn, quinces could be lightly poached or in summer, pitted cherries or berries would be lovely.

CAKES

Spiced Banana Cake

SERVES 6–8

FOR THE CAKE

300 g (10½ oz) self-raising flour

1 teaspoon mixed spice

1 teaspoon ground cinnamon

¼ teaspoon ground cloves

¼ teaspoon ground nutmeg

¼ teaspoon ground ginger

1 teaspoon bicarbonate
of soda (baking soda)

½ teaspoon baking powder

4 eggs

220 g (7¾ oz) white
(granulated) sugar

2 teaspoons finely grated
lemon zest

1 teaspoon finely grated
lime zest

2 teaspoons finely grated
orange zest

650 g (1 lb 7 oz) mashed banana
(see Note)

125 ml (4 fl oz) extra virgin
olive oil

125 g (4½ oz) salted butter, melted

½ teaspoon vanilla extract

FOR THE YOGHURT CREAM

300 ml (10½ fl oz) cream suitable
for whipping

3 teaspoons icing (confectioners')
sugar, or to taste

90 g (3¼ oz) very soft cream cheese

20 g (¾ oz) Greek-style yoghurt

2 teaspoons lemon juice

2 teaspoons lime juice

2 teaspoons orange juice

The secret to this cake's appealing flavour and texture is in the careful blending of spices and citrus with a very generous amount of mashed banana. A yoghurt cream, served separately, provides a delicious contrasting tang, all of which make this cake truly exceptional.

To make the cake

Preheat the oven to 170°C (325°F). Grease an 18 x 25 cm (7 x 10 inch) slab tin, 10 cm (4 inches) deep. Line the base with baking paper and grease again.

Sift together the flour, spices, bicarbonate of soda and baking powder.

Using hand-held beaters or a stand mixer, whisk together the eggs, sugar and citrus zest for 2 minutes.

Make a well in the centre of the dry ingredients and pour this wet mixture in, along with the mashed banana, oil, melted butter and vanilla. Fold together with a large spoon until well combined.

Pour the mixture into the tin, level out, and then bake for 30 minutes, or until a metal skewer inserted into the centre comes out clean.

Leave to stand in the tin for 5 minutes, then turn out onto a wire rack to cool.

To make the yoghurt cream

Using hand-held beaters or a stand mixer, whip the cream with the icing sugar until soft peaks form. Whip in the cream cheese.

Finally, whisk in the yoghurt and citrus juice. The mixture should be a soft peak consistency.

To serve

Serve portions of the cake with a generous dollop of the yoghurt cream.

NOTE *You will need around 1.25 kg (2 lb 12 oz) of ripe bananas to yield enough mashed banana for this recipe. If you find you are just a little short, you can make up the difference with full cream milk or yoghurt.*

Carrot & Pecan Loaf

70 g (2½ oz) softened
  salted butter

80 g (2¾ oz) soft brown sugar

40 ml (1¼ fl oz) maple syrup
  (or golden syrup)

1 teaspoon finely grated
  lemon or lime zest

2 eggs

150 g (5½ oz) self-raising flour

70 g (2½ oz) plain
  (all-purpose) flour

2 teaspoons ground cinnamon

¼ teaspoon ground nutmeg

¼ teaspoon ground cloves

¼ teaspoon bicarbonate
  of soda (baking soda)

300 g (10½ oz) finely grated carrot

60 g (2¼ oz) sultanas

80 g (2¾ oz) pecans, chopped

The moist texture of this loaf contrasts well with the crunch of a generous amount of pecans. It is delicious served sliced and spread with butter.

~~~~~~~

Preheat the oven to 170°C (325°F). Grease a 13 x 20 cm (5 x 8 inch) loaf tin, 7.5 cm (3 inches) deep.

Using hand-held beaters or a stand mixer, whisk together the butter, sugar, maple syrup and zest until light brown in colour. Whisk in the eggs and beat until light and fluffy.

Sift the dry ingredients together and then fold them into the wet mixture with a metal spoon. Fold in the grated carrot, then the sultanas and pecans.

Spoon into the tin, levelling out the surface, and bake for 40 minutes, or until a metal skewer inserted into the centre comes out clean.

Leave to stand in the tin for 10 minutes, then turn out onto a wire rack to cool completely.

Date Custard Column Cake

SERVES 8

½ teaspoon ground nutmeg, for sprinkling

FOR THE CAKE

300 g (10½ oz) pitted dates, chopped

1 teaspoon bicarbonate of soda (baking soda)

375 ml (13 fl oz) boiling water

125 g (4½ oz) softened salted butter

150 g (5½ oz) soft brown sugar

3 eggs

230 g (8½ oz) self-raising flour

FOR THE CUSTARD

650 ml (22½ fl oz) milk

60 g (2¼ oz) custard powder

60 g (2¼ oz) white (granulated) sugar

This cake was invented for the local neighbourhood Wednesday morning tea group who have a great love for custard. So great is this fondness that I have come to call them The Custard Club.

This cake was especially well received as it contains columns of custard inside in addition to its creamy custard topping.

To make the cake

Preheat the oven to 160°C (315°F). Grease a 20 cm (8 inch) square springform cake tin, 8 cm (3¼ inches) deep. Line the base and halfway up the inside with baking paper. Grease again.

Place the chopped dates and bicarbonate of soda into a heatproof bowl and pour the boiling water over. Stir to combine, then leave to stand for 15 minutes.

Pour this mixture into the bowl of a food processor and process until smooth (or blitz with a stick blender).

Using hand-held beaters or a stand mixer, beat the butter and sugar together until well combined and creamy, then add the eggs and beat again. Using a large metal spoon, fold in the flour and the date mixture.

Pour the batter into the tin and bake for 1 hour, or until a metal skewer inserted into the centre comes out clean.

Remove from the oven and leave to stand in the tin for 20 minutes before lifting out of the tin onto the benchtop.

To make the custard

Place the milk in a saucepan and add the custard powder and sugar. Bring to the boil, stirring with a whisk to prevent lumps forming. Simmer for 1 minute, stirring constantly, then remove from the heat.

Place a piece of baking paper on the surface to stop a skin forming.

To assemble the cake

Grease the end of the handle of a wooden spoon and use it to poke holes into the warm cake at regular intervals (around 16 holes is best).

Fill the holes with the warm custard.

Spread the remaining custard over the top and sprinkle with the nutmeg.

Leave to cool before cutting into slices to serve.

The Custard Club

We live on the outskirts of a very small village, tucked away here in the corner of the Derwent Valley. Many of us work from home or have established small businesses here.

One day we received an unexpected text from a neighbour, the gist of which was: 'I am starting a morning tea at my house each Wednesday for those who work at or from home in our township.'

I'd been operating a cooking school on our property for years, so we went along that first morning. There were neighbours there we'd never seen, much less met – with our properties being at least 2 hectares in size, we all lead busy lives.

That first day I'd taken a cake along. It's a habit taught to me by my grandmother, her mantra of sorts: 'When visiting, it's always nice to take a little something delicious to share with others.'

The Wednesday morning tea, a simple cuppa and a slice of cake, has developed a really great dynamic. We know we can call on each other for a hand when and if needed. We watch out for each other. It's certainly an advantage during bushfire season to know who lives where and to be able to check that everyone is safe.

Among the group is a great diversity of work and life skills. It's a pool of knowledge and life experience that is readily shared to others' advantage.

Small kindnesses (and often much larger ones) are commonplace.

For my part, all I can contribute to the equation is an offering of cake each week, which I absolutely love to do.

In that respect, after about a year of these morning teas, someone remarked that they didn't think I'd ever taken the same cake twice. I'd not really thought about it, I just kept on baking, extremely pleased to have such an appreciative audience of taste-testers.

I did like that concept though, and so decided to challenge myself to see if I could keep this going by developing a new sweet treat for them to try each week.

It soon became apparent that including custard in, on, or alongside the cake was very welcome indeed. So much is this the case, and such a constant feature, that I have come to think of the Wednesday morning tea arrangement as 'The Custard Club', a title they don't seem to mind at all.

Sometimes I like to play the game of 'spot the custard' – hiding it in the centre of buns or muffins as a surprise burst of creaminess, or perhaps piped into thick columns within a large cake.

The Wednesday morning tea has become a really significant constant in our neighbourhood and we hate to miss it. It has formed bonds of friendship that will last a lifetime.

For my part, the baking has come to be quite productive, not to mention a great deal of fun. The exercise in developing those new recipes has been instrumental in bringing this book into existence.

Therefore, huge thanks should go to The Custard Club, not only for their taste-testing, inspiration and feedback, but also for being the best friends and neighbours that anyone could ever wish to live among here in this beautiful valley.

Coconut Custard & Passionfruit Ring
(recipe on page 164)

Maple Syrup Upside-Down Banana Cake

SERVES 6–8

FOR THE MAPLE CARAMEL TOPPING

140 g (5 oz) soft brown sugar

60 g (2¼ oz) salted butter

60 ml (2 fl oz) maple syrup

70 g (2½ oz) pecans

500 g (1 lb 2 oz) unpeeled ripe bananas

FOR THE CAKE

100 g (3½ oz) softened salted butter

170 g (6 oz) white (granulated) sugar

1 egg

190 g (6¾ oz) self-raising flour

1 teaspoon ground cinnamon

½ teaspoon mixed spice

½ teaspoon ground ginger

125 ml (4 fl oz) milk

The caramel on this cake is truly exceptional, adding a level of intrigue to the strips of banana that also form part of its topping. The crunch of pecans provides extra texture to the rim of the caramel. The cake itself is a light, spiced butter sponge that is very simple to make and sure to be a favourite.

To make the topping

Preheat the oven to 170°C (325°F). Grease a 20 cm (8 inch) round cake tin, 6 cm (2½ inches) deep. Line the base with baking paper and grease again.

Place the brown sugar, butter and maple syrup in a saucepan and stir over low heat until the sugar is melted and the mixture is well combined – if it separates a little, just whisk vigorously for a minute or two.

Pour into the tin.

Place the pecans in a decorative 8 mm (⅜ inch) wide circle around the circumference of the tin.

Peel the bananas and cut into 5 mm (¼ inch) strips lengthways.

Place the banana strips decoratively over the caramel but not over the rim of nuts.

To make the cake

Using hand-held beaters or a stand mixer, whisk the butter and sugar together until light and fluffy, then add the egg and whisk again.

Combine the flour and spices in a separate bowl then, using a metal spoon, fold them into the butter mixture, alternating with the milk until a smooth batter is formed.

Spoon the batter carefully over the bananas and maple caramel and level out with the back of a wet spoon.

Bake for 30 minutes, or until a metal skewer inserted into the centre comes out clean.

Leave to stand in the tin for 5 minutes before turning out onto a wire rack to cool. Position a plate underneath the rack so that it sits under the cake to catch any drips.

Greek Lemon Syrup Cake

SERVES 6–8

FOR THE CAKE

2 eggs

190 g (6¾ oz) white (granulated) sugar

220 g (7¾ oz) self-raising flour

70 g (2½ oz) Greek-style yoghurt

60 ml (2 fl oz) lemon juice

3 teaspoons finely grated lemon zest

125 g (4½ oz) salted butter, melted

FOR THE SYRUP

180 g (6½ oz) white (granulated) sugar

70 ml (2¼ fl oz) lemon juice

The tang of the lemon and the delightful creaminess of Greek-style yoghurt in this cake is very pronounced and totally delicious. The syrup that is drizzled over the cake after baking lifts the cake's flavour even further.

This is extra special served with crème fraîche or vanilla ice cream.

To make the cake

Preheat the oven to 160°C (315°F). Liberally grease a 20 cm (8 inch) bundt tin. Dust the tin with a thin layer of flour, then turn it over and tap away any excess flour.

Using hand-held beaters or a stand mixer, beat all the cake ingredients for 2 minutes.

Transfer to the tin.

Bake for 30–40 minutes, or until a metal skewer inserted into the cake comes out clean.

Leave to stand in the tin for 5 minutes. During this time, place the tin on a damp tea towel (this helps to release the cake from the tin).

To make the syrup

Place the syrup ingredients and 60 ml (2 fl oz) cold water into a small saucepan and bring to the boil over medium heat, stirring. Once boiling, turn the heat to medium–low and cook for 3–5 minutes without stirring, to thicken slightly.

To serve

Invert the cake onto a serving platter and prick all over with a skewer at 1 cm (½ inch) intervals.

Pour the hot syrup over the warm cake.

Serve warm or cold.

Chocolate Beetroot Cake

SERVES 8

This cake was hastily put together during a talkback radio segment when a caller with an excess of beetroot needed a recipe. I thought it would work, but raced home afterwards and immediately put it to the test. It turned out to be a very successful recipe.

~~~~~~

FOR THE CAKE

60 g (2¼ oz) dark chocolate, broken into small pieces, or dark chocolate melts

50 ml (1½ fl oz) pouring cream or evaporated milk

2 eggs

200 g (7 oz) white (granulated) sugar

125 ml (4 fl oz) milk

220 g (7¾ oz) self-raising flour

30 g (1 oz) cocoa

½ teaspoon baking powder

90 g (3¼ oz) salted butter, melted

80 g (2¾ oz) finely grated raw beetroot or puréed cooked beetroot or drained puréed tinned beetroot (no need to rinse the vinegar from it)

FOR THE ICING

2 teaspoons softened salted butter, diced

90 g (3¼ oz) dark chocolate, broken into small pieces, or dark chocolate melts

60 ml (2 fl oz) pouring cream or evaporated milk

100 g (3½ oz) icing (confectioners') sugar, sifted

To make the cake

Preheat the oven to 160°C (315°F). Grease a 20 cm (8 inch) round cake tin, 7 cm (2¾ inches) deep. Line the base with baking paper and grease again.

Place the chocolate in a small heatproof bowl. Bring the cream or evaporated milk to boiling point and then pour it over the chocolate. Leave to stand for 3 minutes, and then stir to melt the chocolate. Set aside and stir every now and then so it does not set.

Using hand-held beaters or a stand mixer, mix together the eggs, sugar, milk, flour, cocoa, baking powder and melted butter. Beat for 2 minutes, then add the melted chocolate mixture and beat for 1 minute more.

Using a large metal spoon, fold in the beetroot until thoroughly combined.

Pour into the tin and smooth out the top.

Bake for 30–40 minutes, or until a metal skewer inserted into the centre comes out clean.

Leave to stand in the tin for 5 minutes, then turn out onto a wire rack to cool completely.

To make the icing

Place the butter and chocolate in a small heatproof bowl. Bring the cream or evaporated milk to boiling point and then pour it over the butter and chocolate. Leave to stand for 3 minutes, and then stir to melt the chocolate and butter.

Leave the mixture to cool, then whisk in the icing sugar.

Spread over the cooled cake and leave to set before cutting.

Slices &
Tray Bakes

Lemon & Lavender Slice

SERVES 8–12

1 teaspoon icing
(confectioners') sugar,
for dusting

1 teaspoon dried
culinary-use lavender
buds, for sprinkling

FOR THE LAVENDER SUGAR

350 g (12 oz) white
(granulated) sugar

5 teaspoons dried culinary-use
lavender buds

FOR THE BASE

180 g (6½ oz) very soft
salted butter

50 g (1¾ oz) lavender sugar

290 g (10¼ oz) plain
(all-purpose) flour

½ teaspoon baking powder

FOR THE FILLING

5 eggs

150 ml (5 fl oz) lemon juice

300 g (10½ oz) lavender sugar

2 teaspoons finely grated
lemon zest

30 g (1 oz) cornflour
(cornstarch)

There are many varieties of lavender, but a great number are not suitable for cooking and eating as they are heavily camphorous. Amongst the best edible varieties is *Lavandula angustifolia*. When used sparingly, the flavour is intriguing and pleasant, adding a subtle interest to sweet dishes such as this one.

This slice is an old-fashioned favourite, and deserves to be moved into your contemporary baking repertoire, as it is one of the most stunning sweet treats you can ever wish to make.

~~~~~~~~

To make the lavender sugar

Place 200 g (7 oz) of the sugar and the lavender in the bowl of a food processor and process until the lavender is finely chopped. Add the remaining sugar to the processor and process for 1 minute more.

You can make this in advance and store it in an airtight container in the refrigerator (it will keep for up to 3 weeks).

To make the base

Preheat the oven to 160°C (315°F). Grease a 22 x 35 cm (8½ x 14 inch) slab tin, 5 cm (2 inches) deep, and line the base and part way up the sides with baking paper. Grease again.

Using a hand whisk, mix the butter and lavender sugar until pale.

In a separate bowl, combine the flour and baking powder, then add to the butter mixture and mix until well combined.

Press evenly into the tin.

Bake for 20 minutes, or until light golden brown.

To make the filling

In a large bowl, whisk together the eggs, lemon juice, lavender sugar, lemon zest and cornflour until smooth.

To assemble

When the base is cooked, remove it from the oven and while it is still hot, carefully pour the filling mixture on top. Return to the oven and bake for a further 20 minutes, or until the filling is set.

Leave in the tin to cool completely before dusting with the icing sugar and sprinkling the lavender buds over the top. Cut into squares to serve.

Mocha Slice

SERVES 8–12

FOR THE BASE

2 eggs

200 g (7 oz) white
  (granulated) sugar

180 ml (6 fl oz) milk

200 g (7 oz) self-raising flour

2 teaspoons cocoa

40 ml (1¼ fl oz) coffee
  and chicory essence

90 g (3¼ oz) salted butter,
  melted

FOR THE ICING

230 g (8½ oz) icing
  (confectioners') sugar, sifted

1 teaspoon instant coffee powder
  or granules, dissolved in
  2 teaspoons hot water

1½ teaspoons coffee
  and chicory essence

2 teaspoons salted butter,
  melted

3 teaspoons boiling water,
  plus extra if needed

2 teaspoons cocoa

With its pretty feather-and-fan pattern comprised of both chocolate and coffee flavours, this slice is delicious as a morning or afternoon tea treat. Old-fashioned coffee and chicory essence is used in this cake – it doesn't dry out the cake like some other types of coffee flavouring can. The essence is readily available at supermarkets.

~~~~~~~~~

To make the base

Preheat the oven to 170°C (325°F). Grease an 18 x 28 cm (7 x 11¼ inch) slab tin, 5 cm (2 inches) deep. Line the base with baking paper and grease again.

Place all the ingredients in a bowl, melted butter last, and beat using hand-held beaters or a stand mixer for 2 minutes.

Pour the mixture into the tin and bake for 25 minutes, or until a metal skewer inserted into the centre comes out clean.

Leave to stand in the tin for 5 minutes, then turn out onto a wire rack to cool completely.

To make the icing

To make the coffee icing, stir all the icing ingredients (except the cocoa) together in a heatproof bowl. If needed, stir in a little more boiling water (a few drops at a time) until a spreading consistency is reached.

To make the chocolate icing for piping, place 2 tablespoons of the coffee icing into another heatproof bowl, add the cocoa and a little boiling water (a few drops at a time) and stir until a spreading consistency is reached.

Spread the coffee icing on the cake, then pipe thin lines of the chocolate icing over the top, spaced at 1 cm (½ inch) intervals.

Drag a skewer through, first in one direction and then the other, again at 1 cm intervals.

Leave to stand for at least 15 minutes to set before cutting and serving.

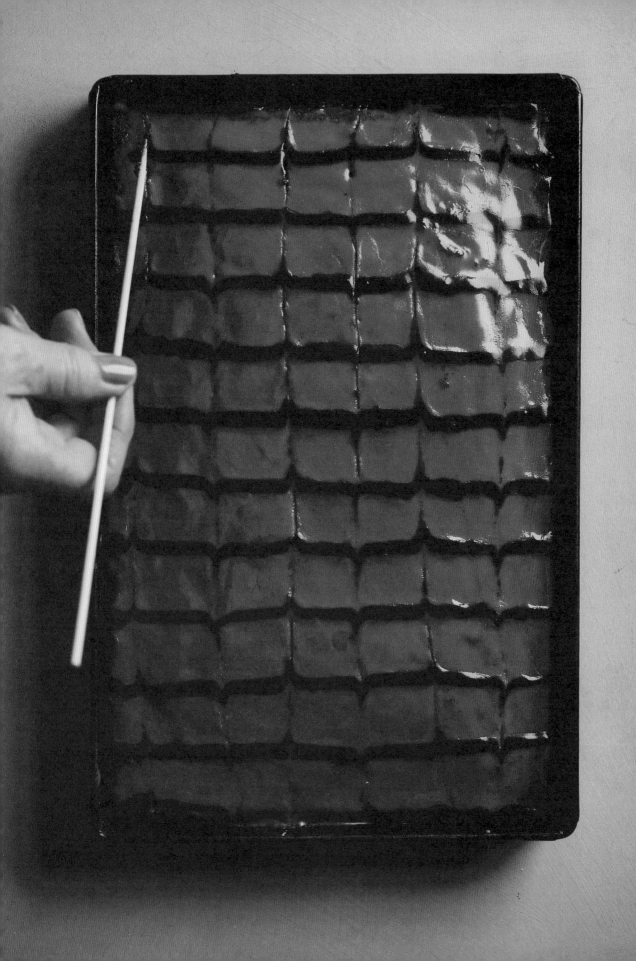

Apricot & Blueberry Tray Bake

SERVES 8–12

2 eggs

250 g (9 oz) white (granulated) sugar, plus 1½ teaspoons extra

2 teaspoons finely grated lemon zest

320 ml (11 fl oz) milk

60 ml (2 fl oz) lemon juice

440 g (15½ oz) self-raising flour

125 g (4½ oz) salted butter, melted, plus 40 g (1½ oz) extra

800 g (1 lb 12 oz) apricot halves, drained if tinned

180 g (6½ oz) blueberries, fresh or frozen

1 teaspoon ground cinnamon

Apricots are certainly one of my favourite stone fruits. They are so obliging, making sensational jam and beautiful preserves and never failing to turn a simple plain cake into something really special. Here, blueberries are included for their colour, flavour and 'pop' of texture. The tray bake is finished with butter, cinnamon and sugar, like a teacake.

You can use fresh, tinned or preserved apricots and fresh or frozen blueberries in this easy bake.

~~~~~~~~~

Preheat the oven to 160°C (315°F). Grease a 24 x 35 cm (9½ x 14 inch) baking dish, 10 cm (4 inches) deep.

Using hand-held beaters or a stand mixer, whisk the eggs, the 250 g (9 oz) sugar and the lemon zest together until creamy. Add the milk, lemon juice, flour and the 125 g (4½ oz) melted butter. Whisk briefly until smooth.

Transfer to the dish and smooth out the surface.

Place the apricots and blueberries decoratively over the top.

Bake for 30 minutes, or until a metal skewer inserted into the centre comes out clean.

Remove from the oven and brush with the extra melted butter. Combine the extra sugar with the cinnamon and sprinkle over the top.

Cut and serve straight from the tin.

Apricots

Apricots are my favourite stone fruit of summer. I adore preserving them – for cakes, puddings and even savoury dishes throughout the year.

I have a particular preference for an older variety, Moorpark, which is enthusiastically sought after by all avid bottlers. When these apricots are preserved by the waterbath method they retain their texture and flavour and so are perfect for baking when needed.

Recently my usual source informed me they no longer grew them; yet another had removed more than half from their orchard and no longer sold to the public. What was I to do? A summer without apricots was unthinkable.

Rescue came in the form of an extensive orchard in the Coal River Valley near the township of Campania, an area not too far away where they specialise in growing this variety.

I contacted the owner regularly for weeks, waiting – none too patiently – until the harvest came around. When the day finally arrived, we travelled out there immediately and bought 40 kg (88 lb) of perfect fruit for bottling. Within a day they were in the jars, halves preserved in light syrup, and made into unsweetened purée for crumbles, pies and tarts.

A few days later I was running a bottling class so we headed out again to get 20 kg (44 lb) more. A large Apricot & Blueberry Tray Bake was prepared for the participants to enjoy for morning tea (see recipe page 82).

I am very much in favour of fruit in cakes and desserts – as evidenced by the number of recipes that include them. They not only add flavour, texture and interest, but also the bonus of heightened nutritional value.

Chocolate & Raspberry Cheesecake Slice

SERVES 8–12

FOR THE BASE

125 g (4½ oz) very soft salted butter

125 g (4½ oz) white (granulated) sugar

1 egg, lightly whisked

220 g (7¾ oz) self-raising flour

30 g (1 oz) cocoa, sifted

FOR THE FILLING

200 g (7 oz) soft ricotta

250 g (9 oz) cream cheese, softened

250 g (9 oz) white (granulated) sugar

125 g (4½ oz) sour cream

120 ml (4 fl oz) lemon juice

2 teaspoons finely grated lemon zest

6 eggs

30 g (1 oz) cornflour (cornstarch)

350 g (12 oz) raspberries

This has it all – the decadence of chocolate shortcake, the fresh tang of raspberries and a sumptuous lemon cream filling that brings the whole together. Undoubtedly it is one of my most popular slices – a touch of luxury to share with friends. It is surprisingly easy to make and the result is simply stunning.

Here in the Derwent Valley, berries abound. After all, it's been a fruit-growing region since colonial times and the quality is excellent due to the cool temperate climate, which allows slow maturation, followed by summer days of searing heat, which takes the flavour of the berries to an exquisite level.

Raspberries are an all-time favourite, but loganberries, mulberries (if you can get them), blackberries or blueberries could be substituted. Fresh or frozen berries can be used in this recipe.

~~~~~~~~~

To make the base

Preheat the oven to 170°C (325°F). Grease a 26 cm (10½ inch) square springform cake tin, 8 cm (3¼ inches) deep.

Using a hand whisk, mix the butter and sugar together until creamy, then add the egg and whisk again until combined. In a separate bowl, combine the flour and cocoa then, using a large metal spoon, fold the dry ingredients into the butter mixture until well blended.

Press evenly into the tin and bake for 10 minutes until the base is set. Set aside to cool while making the filling.

Reduce the oven temperature to 130°C (250°F).

To make the filling

Place all the ingredients except the raspberries in the bowl of a food processor and process until smooth. (This could also be done with hand-held beaters or a stand mixer.) Transfer to a bowl.

Gently mix 300 g (10½ oz) of the raspberries through the mixture.

Carefully spoon the batter onto the cooled base.

Scatter the remaining raspberries over the top.

Bake for 1 hour, or until the topping is just set. Leave to cool and then refrigerate to firm up the filling.

When you're ready to serve, run a warm knife around the slice before releasing the side of the pan (this will ensure it comes away cleanly). Cut into squares to serve.

Lemon Chiffon Tray Bake

SERVES 8–12

This is an exceptionally delicious light and airy bake perfect for sharing. The lemon is enhanced by a cream-cheese icing swirled with lemon curd. Of course you can buy lemon curd but making your own makes this just a bit more special. The leftovers can be stored in a sterilised jar in the fridge for up to 10 days.

~~~~~~~

FOR THE BASE

250 g (9 oz) self-raising flour

3 teaspoons baking powder

¼ teaspoon sea salt

300 g (10½ oz) white (granulated) sugar

60 ml (2 fl oz) milk

6 egg yolks

125 ml (4 fl oz) vegetable oil

1 tablespoon finely grated lemon zest

120 ml (4 fl oz) lemon juice

8 egg whites

½ teaspoon cream of tartar

FOR THE LEMON CURD

3½ teaspoons cornflour (cornstarch)

150 ml (5 fl oz) lemon juice

5 teaspoons finely grated lemon zest

2 eggs, plus 2 egg yolks, lightly whisked

200 g (7 oz) white (granulated) sugar

150 g (5½ oz) salted butter, diced

To make the base

Preheat the oven to 170°C (325°F). Grease a 22 x 35 x 4 cm (8½ x 14 x 1½ inch) lamington-style tin.

In a large bowl, sift together the flour, baking powder and salt, then stir in the sugar.

In a separate bowl, whisk together the milk, egg yolks, oil, lemon zest and juice until well combined.

Make a well in the centre of the dry ingredients and then pour in the liquid mixture. Beat for 2 minutes using hand-held beaters or a stand mixer, then set aside.

In a separate and very clean large bowl, whisk the egg whites with the cream of tartar with hand-held beaters or a stand mixer until glossy peaks form.

Use a metal spoon to fold the egg whites in four batches into the cake batter.

Spoon the batter evenly into the tin and bake for 30–35 minutes until the cake pulls away from the sides a little and a metal skewer inserted into the centre comes out clean.

Leave to cool completely.

To make the lemon curd

Combine the cornflour and lemon juice, then place in a small saucepan with the remaining ingredients.

Whisk over low heat for 10 minutes until the mixture thickens. Strain through a sieve and allow to cool.

This makes 280 g (10 oz). You'll only need about a third of this for the slice; keep the rest for another time, to top freshly baked scones or fill little tart cases.

FOR THE TOPPING

180 g (6½ oz) cream cheese,
  softened

60 g (2¼ oz) softened
  salted butter

3 teaspoons finely grated
  lemon zest

350 g (12 oz) icing
  (confectioners') sugar

40 ml (1¼ fl oz) lemon juice

To make the topping

Whisk together the cream cheese and butter until well combined.
Use a large metal spoon to stir in the zest and icing sugar, adding
lemon juice as needed to make a soft, spreadable icing.

Spread over the top of the cooled cake.

To assemble

Make small indents in the icing and spoon over the lemon curd
to taste, swirling to make a decorative pattern.

Cut into squares and serve straight from the tin.

Lemon Chiffon Tray Bake
(recipe on pages 88–9)

Nectarine Crumble Tray Bake
(recipe on page 92)

Nectarine Crumble Tray Bake

SERVES 8–12

1 egg white, lightly whisked

FOR THE FILLING

900 g (2 lb) nectarines, stones removed and flesh cut into small cubes

60 g (2¼ oz) white (granulated) sugar, or to taste

3 teaspoons lemon juice

3 teaspoons cornflour (cornstarch) mixed to a paste with 40 ml (1¼ fl oz) cold water

FOR THE PASTRY

125 g (4½ oz) very soft salted butter

200 g (7 oz) white (granulated) sugar

2 eggs

300 g (10½ oz) plain (all-purpose) flour

150 g (5½ oz) self-raising flour

1 teaspoon bicarbonate of soda (baking soda)

FOR THE CRUMBLE

15 g (½ oz) cold salted butter, diced

40 g (1½ oz) self-raising flour

55 g (2 oz) soft brown sugar

Last summer a kind neighbour invited us to pick the last of the nectarine crop from her trees. 'There'll just be about half a bucketful', she said – such a humble understatement of her generosity. We came away with more than two buckets filled to overflowing. I bottled many, with pies, crumbles and tarts in mind. This recipe is a combination of all three: a crostata-type slice covered with lattice pastry and topped with crumble. While almost any fruit could be used in this recipe, nectarines or peaches are especially delicious.

~~~~~~

To make the filling

Place the nectarine and sugar into a saucepan with 60 ml (2 fl oz) water, bring to the boil, then reduce the heat and simmer until the fruit is just tender. Stir in the lemon juice.

While still simmering, gradually stir in enough cornflour paste to reach a thick custard consistency. Set aside to cool.

To make the pastry

Using a hand whisk, mix the butter and sugar together until creamy, then whisk in the eggs until well combined. In a separate bowl, mix the dry ingredients together then, using a large metal spoon, fold them through the egg mixture until well combined. Wrap in plastic wrap and place in the fridge for at least 30 minutes to firm up before using.

To make the crumble

Place the ingredients in a food processor and process until the mixture resembles breadcrumbs. (Alternatively, this can be achieved by rubbing the ingredients together with your fingers.) Set aside.

To assemble for baking

Preheat the oven to 170°C (325°F). Grease a 22 x 35 cm (8½ x 14 inch) slab tin, 8 cm (3¼ inches) deep. Cut one-third from the pastry, cover and set aside.

On a lightly floured surface, roll out the remaining pastry to the size of the tin and press into the sides and edges. Brush with some of the whisked egg white to seal. Spread the cooled fruit mixture over this. Roll out the reserved pastry and cut into long strips about 1 cm (½ inch) wide. Place these in a lattice pattern over the top of the fruit.

Sprinkle the crumble mixture into the spaces between the lattice strips. Bake for 30 minutes, or until it is nicely browned.

Leave to stand in the tin for at least 30 minutes before cutting into squares to serve.

Fruit 'n' Nut Slice

SERVES 8–12

150 g (5½ oz) wholemeal
self-raising flour

180 g (6½ oz) raw sugar

½ large apple, coarsely grated

90 g (3¼ oz) pitted dates, chopped

80 g (2¾ oz) desiccated coconut

80 g (2¾ oz) walnuts or
pecans, chopped

50 g (1¾ oz) sultanas

50 g (1¾ oz) dried cranberries

60 g (2¼ oz) dried apricots,
diced

70 g (2½ oz) pepitas
(pumpkin seeds)

1 teaspoon mixed spice

1 teaspoon ground cinnamon

½ teaspoon vanilla extract

2 large eggs, whisked

100 g (3½ oz) salted butter,
melted

This slice is bursting with the goodness and flavour of dried fruits, spices and nutty wholemeal flour. It's ideal for children to help prepare and certainly wholesome for them to eat as a snack.

Preheat the oven to 160°C (315°F). Grease an 18 x 28 cm (7 x 11¼ inch) slab tin, 6 cm (2½ inches) deep.

Mix all the ingredients together with a metal spoon, then press evenly into the tin and flatten with the back of a spoon.

Bake for 25 minutes until golden.

Cool before cutting into squares to serve straight from the tin.

Rhubarb & Caramel Slice

SERVES 8–12

FOR THE PASTRY

125 g (4½ oz) very
   soft salted butter

125 g (4½ oz) white
   (granulated) sugar,
   or to taste

1 egg

½ teaspoon vanilla extract

100 g (3½ oz) plain
   (all-purpose) flour

150 g (5½ oz) self-raising flour

FOR THE FILLING

750 g (1 lb 10 oz) rhubarb stalks

100 g (3½ oz) white
   (granulated) sugar,
   or more to taste

3 teaspoons lemon juice

2 teaspoons cornflour
   (cornstarch) mixed to
   a paste with 40 ml (1¼ fl oz)
   cold water

FOR THE TOPPING

90 g (3¼ oz) salted butter

90 ml (3 fl oz) milk

30 ml (1 fl oz) lemon juice

210 g (7½ oz) soft brown sugar

100 g (3½ oz) shredded coconut

Since we fenced our rhubarb, the possums can no longer eat it right down to the ground and nowadays we have an abundance. I have found there is no better way to use it up than by preparing this treat to share with friends.

Lovely, dusky earthy flavours come together in this slice with its butter shortcake base and a topping of shredded caramel coconut.

To make the pastry

Whisk the butter and sugar together until pale. Whisk in the egg and vanilla until creamy.

Sift the flours together in a separate bowl then, using a large metal spoon, fold into the butter mixture until well combined.

Wrap in plastic wrap and place in the fridge for at least 30 minutes to firm up before using.

To make the filling

Trim the ends of the rhubarb and then cut the stalks into 2.5 cm (1 inch) lengths.

Place the rhubarb and sugar in a saucepan with 60 ml (2 fl oz) water, bring to the boil and then reduce the heat to low and simmer for 10 minutes, or until just tender. Add the lemon juice and gradually stir in enough cornflour paste to reach a thick custard consistency. Taste and add more sugar if needed.

Set aside to cool.

To make the topping

Combine all the ingredients in a saucepan and bring to the boil, stirring. Simmer for 2 minutes, stirring constantly, until the butter and sugar have melted.

To assemble for baking

Preheat the oven to 170°C (325°F). Grease a 23 x 35 cm (9 x 14 inch) baking dish, 8 cm (3¼ inches) deep.

On a lightly floured surface, roll out the pastry to the size of the baking dish and press into place.

Spread the cooled rhubarb mixture over this. Spoon the topping over the rhubarb.

Bake for 35 minutes until nicely browned.

Leave to stand in the tin for 30 minutes before cutting and serving straight from the tin.

Lemon Blossom Slice

FOR THE BASE

3 eggs

300 g (10½ oz) white (granulated) sugar

60 ml (2 fl oz) lemon juice

1 tablespoon finely grated lemon zest

440 g (15½ oz) self-raising flour

125 ml (4 fl oz) vegetable oil or light olive oil

FOR THE LEMON CURD FILLING

15 g (½ oz) cornflour (cornstarch)

80 ml (2½ fl oz) lemon juice

finely grated zest of 2 large lemons

3 eggs, lightly whisked

190 g (6¾ oz) white (granulated) sugar

125 g (4½ oz) salted butter, diced

FOR THE MARSHMALLOW

250 g (9 oz) white (granulated) sugar

15 g (½ oz) gelatine powder

60 ml (2 fl oz) lemon juice

This delicious slice is named for its bold and beautiful colours which are reminiscent of the swathes of yellow wattle that surround our property each spring.

Celebrating the flavour of lemon with a buttery sponge and lemon curd filling, this rich and tasty sweet treat is finished with a layer of airy marshmallow.

~~~~~~

To make the base

Preheat the oven to 170°C (325°F). Grease a 20 x 30 cm (8 x 12 inch) slab tin, 6 cm (2½ inches) deep. Line the base with baking paper and grease again.

Using hand-held beaters or a stand mixer, whisk the eggs and sugar until light and fluffy.

Add the lemon juice, zest, flour, oil and 330 ml (11¼ fl oz) cold water, then fold together with a large metal spoon until smooth.

Pour into the tin, smooth out the top and bake for 30 minutes, or until a metal skewer inserted into the centre comes out clean.

Leave to stand for 5 minutes, then invert onto a wire rack to cool.

To make the lemon curd filling

Mix the cornflour with the lemon juice, then place with all the ingredients in a small saucepan.

Whisk over low heat until the mixture thickens.

Strain through a sieve.

Place a piece of baking paper on the surface to stop a skin forming, then refrigerate to cool completely, stirring occasionally.

To make the marshmallow

In a saucepan, mix the sugar, gelatine and lemon juice together, then stir in 375 ml (13 fl oz) cold water. Bring to the boil, stirring constantly, then reduce the heat to medium–low and simmer for 12 minutes, stirring occasionally.

Remove from the heat and cool, but do not allow it to set. (If it does, simply place the saucepan back over low heat until it melts again.)

recipe continued overleaf

Lemon Blossom Slice . . . cont'd

To assemble

Place the cooled base on a suitable platter. Cut out a shallow recess, scooping out the crumb, and leaving a 1 cm (½ inch) rim around the outside.

Fill the recess with the lemon curd filling and smooth out.

Now it's time to whip the marshmallow. Beat using hand-held beaters or a stand mixer until thick and white and it holds its peaks.

Spread the whipped marshmallow on top of the filling and leave to set.

To serve

Cut the slice into portions with a knife that has been dipped in hot water, then wiped dry.

Ginger & Rum Syrup Slice

SERVES 8–12

FOR THE SLICE

220 g (7¾ oz) very soft salted butter

200 g (7 oz) soft brown sugar

250 g (9 oz) treacle

3 eggs

320 g (11¼ oz) self-raising flour

3 teaspoons cocoa

4 teaspoons ground ginger

2 teaspoons mixed spice

2 teaspoons ground cinnamon

¼ teaspoon ground cloves

¼ teaspoon ground cardamom

¼ teaspoon ground nutmeg

60 ml (2 fl oz) pouring cream

2 teaspoons lime or lemon juice

80 ml (2½ fl oz) rum

80 g (2¾ oz) crystallised or glacé ginger, roughly chopped

FOR THE SYRUP

130 ml (4 fl oz) rum

100 g (3½ oz) white (granulated) sugar

1 tablespoon coarsely grated fresh young ginger

¼ teaspoon mixed spice

¼ teaspoon ground cinnamon

pinch of ground nutmeg

pinch of ground cloves

pinch of ground cardamom

While this is delicious served as a cut-and-come-again slice, it is also delightful served as a dessert with crème fraîche.

To make the slice

Preheat the oven to 160°C (315°F). Grease a 20 x 25 cm (8 x 10 inch) slab tin, 6 cm (2½ inches) deep.

In a large bowl, use a hand whisk to mix the butter, sugar and treacle together until light and fluffy, then whisk in the eggs one at a time.

In a separate bowl, sift in the dry ingredients, then fold into the wet ingredients with a large metal spoon. Finally, fold in the cream, lime or lemon juice, rum and crystallised or glacé ginger.

Transfer to the tin.

Bake for 40 minutes, or until a metal skewer inserted into the centre comes out clean.

Leave to cool for 15 minutes.

To make the syrup

Place all the syrup ingredients and 50 ml (1½ fl oz) water in a small saucepan. Bring to the boil, stirring, then simmer for 10 minutes without stirring.

Remove from the heat, allow to cool for 5 minutes, then strain out the ginger.

To assemble

Pierce the cooled slice at 8 mm (⅜ inch) intervals with a skewer and then drizzle the syrup over the top.

Leave to infuse for at least 20 minutes before cutting into squares or slices to serve straight from the tin.

Coconut Crunch Apple Slice

SERVES 8–12

1 egg white, lightly whisked

FOR THE PASTRY BASE

125 g (4½ oz) very soft
   salted butter

85 g (3 oz) white
   (granulated) sugar

1 egg

10 g (¼ oz) wholemeal
   self-raising flour

60 g (2¼ oz) plain
   (all-purpose) flour

70 g (2½ oz) self-raising flour

FOR THE FILLING

600 g (1 lb 5 oz) apples such as
   granny smith or golden delicious,
   peeled, cored and diced

30 g (1 oz) white (granulated)
   sugar, or to taste

3 teaspoons lemon juice

3 teaspoons custard powder
   mixed to a paste with
   30 ml (1 fl oz) cold water

FOR THE TOPPING

3 eggs

120 g (4¼ oz) white
   (granulated) sugar

110 g (3¾ oz) desiccated coconut

50 g (1¾ oz) salted butter, melted

½ teaspoon vanilla extract

Here, apples are made special by a crunchy coconut topping, which develops a lovely deep brown gloss as it bakes.

To make the pastry base

Using a hand whisk, mix the butter and sugar together until well combined, then whisk in the egg until creamy.

In a separate bowl, combine the flours then, using a large metal spoon, fold into the butter mixture. Cover and set aside.

To make the filling

Place the apple, sugar, lemon juice and 100 ml (3½ fl oz) water in a saucepan and bring to the boil, stirring. Reduce the heat and simmer until the apple is just tender.

Thicken with some or all of the custard powder paste if needed. The filling should become a thick custard consistency. Cool completely before using.

To make the topping

Whisk together the eggs and sugar, and then mix in the coconut, melted butter and vanilla.

To assemble for baking

Preheat the oven to 170°C (325°F). Grease an 18 x 28 x 4 cm (7 x 11¼ x 1½ inch) lamington-style tin.

Roll the pastry out to fit the base of the tin.

Press the pastry evenly into the tin and then brush with some of the whisked egg white to seal.

Spread with the cooled apple filling.

Spoon the topping over the filling and even out with the back of a damp spoon.

Bake for 30 minutes, or until golden brown and the topping is set.

Cut and serve straight from the tin.

Loch Katrine Slice

SERVES 12–16

60 g (2¼ oz) desiccated coconut

FOR THE BASE

150 g (5½ oz) plain
   (all-purpose) flour

1 teaspoon baking powder

70 g (2½ oz) cold salted
   butter, diced

1 egg, separated

250 g (9 oz) raspberry jam

80 g (2¾ oz) currants

FOR THE SPONGE

1 egg

170 g (6 oz) white
   (granulated) sugar

1 teaspoon finely grated
   lemon zest

220 g (7¾ oz) self-raising flour

180 ml (6 fl oz) milk

70 g (2½ oz) salted butter,
   melted

FOR THE ICING

250 g (9 oz) icing
   (confectioners') sugar

1½ teaspoons softened
   salted butter

½ teaspoon vanilla extract

few drops pink
   food colouring

30 ml (1 fl oz) boiling water

As the name might well suggest, this sweet treat originated in Scotland. This old-fashioned favourite consists of a layer of pastry, then raspberry jam, dried currants and a buttery sponge, all finished with pink icing and coconut.

~~~~~~~

To make the base

Preheat the oven to 170°C (325°F). Grease an 18 x 28 cm (7 x 11¼ inch) slab tin, 6 cm (2½ inches) deep and line the base with baking paper. Grease again.

Place the flour, baking powder and butter in a food processor and pulse until the mixture resembles breadcrumbs. (Alternatively, this can be achieved by rubbing the ingredients together with your fingers.) Transfer to a large bowl.

In a small bowl, whisk the egg yolk and 50 ml (1½ fl oz) water together. Add this to the large bowl and mix to form a soft dough.

Whisk the egg white in another small bowl. Press the dough evenly into the tin, then brush with some of the whisked egg white to seal. Spread with a layer of raspberry jam, then sprinkle with the currants.

To make the sponge

Using hand-held beaters or a stand mixer, whisk the egg, sugar and lemon zest until well combined and pale. Add the flour, milk and butter and whisk until smooth.

Spoon the batter evenly over the currants.

Bake for 25–30 minutes, or until a skewer inserted into the centre comes out clean.

Allow to stand in the tin for 5 minutes before turning out onto a wire rack to cool completely.

To make the icing

Sift the icing sugar into a bowl. Add the butter, vanilla, a few drops of pink colouring and enough of the boiling water to make a good spreading consistency.

Spread the icing over the cake and sprinkle with the coconut.

Cut into squares when set.

Simple Sultana & Walnut Slice

SERVES 8–12

125 g (4½ oz) salted butter

200 g (7 oz) white (granulated) sugar

2 teaspoons ground cinnamon

1 teaspoon mixed spice

¼ teaspoon ground cloves

375 g (13 oz) sultanas

1 teaspoon bicarbonate of soda (baking soda)

2 eggs

150 g (5½ oz) plain (all-purpose) flour

150 g (5½ oz) self-raising flour

125 g (4½ oz) walnuts, roughly chopped

This is moist and flavoursome, full of the sweet softness of sultanas with a complementary crunch of walnuts. It can be cut into 1 cm (½ inch) slices and buttered, or served in squares as is.

Place the butter, sugar, spices, sultanas, bicarbonate of soda and 260 ml (9 fl oz) water in a large saucepan.

Bring to the boil, stirring, then reduce the heat and simmer for 1 minute.

Remove from the heat and allow to cool for 15 minutes.

Preheat the oven to 160°C (315°F). Grease a 25 x 35 cm (10 x 14 inch) slab tin, 8 cm (3¼ inches) deep.

Whisk the eggs and add to the sultana mixture, then add the flours and mix with a metal spoon until well combined. Fold in the walnuts, then pour the mixture into the tin.

Bake for 30 minutes, or until a metal skewer inserted into the centre comes out clean.

Allow to cool in the tin, then slice and serve.

Fabulous
Finishes

~

Old-Fashioned Custard Tart

SERVES 6–8

1 egg white, whisked

½ teaspoon ground nutmeg

FOR THE PASTRY

125 g (4½ oz) very soft salted butter

125 g (4½ oz) white (granulated) sugar

1 egg

150 g (5½ oz) plain (all-purpose) flour

100 g (3½ oz) self-raising flour

FOR THE FILLING

1.125 litres (39½ fl oz) milk

1 teaspoon vanilla extract

110 g (3¾ oz) cornflour (cornstarch)

6 egg yolks

2 eggs

100 g (3½ oz) white (granulated) sugar

2 teaspoons lemon juice

NOTE *Any trimmings from the pastry can be refrigerated for up to 2 weeks or frozen for 2 months.*

This has to be one of the most popular desserts of all time: thick custard sprinkled with nutmeg in a crisp sweet shortcrust pastry. In keeping with the style of this old-fashioned favourite, the custard in this tart is made from scratch. It is partially cooked on the stovetop before being spooned into the pastry case. This eliminates the risk of custard seeping through the crust and making the base soggy.

To make the pastry

Using a hand whisk, combine the butter and sugar together in a large bowl, then whisk in the egg until creamy. In a separate bowl, combine the flours then, using a large metal spoon, fold into the butter mixture to make a soft dough. Wrap in plastic wrap and place in the fridge for at least 30 minutes to firm up before using.

To make the filling

Heat 1 litre (35 fl oz) of the milk and the vanilla in a large saucepan to boiling point.

Meanwhile, in a heatproof bowl, whisk together the cornflour and the remaining 125 ml (4 fl oz) milk. Add the egg yolks, eggs and sugar and whisk until completely free of lumps. Gradually pour 125 ml (4 fl oz) of the hot milk from the pan into the egg mixture, whisking, then add another 125 ml (4 fl oz). Once incorporated, tip all the egg mixture into the remaining milk in the saucepan and cook over medium–low heat until thickened, whisking constantly. Remove from the heat and stir in the lemon juice.

Place a piece of baking paper on the surface to stop a skin forming, then set aside to cool completely.

To assemble for baking

Preheat the oven to 200°C (400°F). Grease a 23 cm (9 inch) round flan tin or tart plate, 8 cm (3¼ inches) deep.

On a lightly floured surface, roll out the dough to 6 mm (¼ inch) thick.

Press the pastry evenly into the tin and then brush with some of the whisked egg white to seal. If the pastry breaks as you are lifting it in, just patch it back together in the tin. Trim the top of the pastry above the rim if needed. Leave to stand for 5 minutes.

Spoon in the cooled custard and sprinkle with the nutmeg. Bake for 10 minutes. Reduce the oven temperature to 140°C (275°F) and bake for a further 30 minutes, or until the filling is set. Cool on a wire rack and then refrigerate until firm enough to cut cleanly.

Rhubarb Jelly Flan

SERVES 6–8

whipped cream, to serve

FOR THE BASE

1 egg

170 g (6 oz) white (granulated) sugar

180 ml (6 fl oz) milk

230 g (8½ oz) self-raising flour

80 g (2¾ oz) salted butter, melted

FOR THE FILLING

300 g (11 oz) rhubarb stalks, ends trimmed

20 g (¾ oz) white (granulated) sugar

85 g (3 oz) packet strawberry jelly crystals

375 ml (13 fl oz) boiling water

Rhubarb is a staple in our vegetable patch. While I make many preserves with it, I also like to bake this tasty flan for the grandchildren, who have a great liking for jelly. However, it is well accepted anywhere by young and old alike.

This flan can be made a day ahead of time and pulled out of the fridge to serve as a centrepiece – pretty enough to impress any friend or family member.

I use preserved rhubarb pieces if I have them on hand, otherwise I roast the rhubarb – it's simple to do and the rhubarb keeps its shape well.

To make the base

Preheat the oven to 160°C (315°F). Grease a 23 cm (9 inch) recessed fluted flan tin and line the base with baking paper. Grease again.

Using hand-held beaters or a stand mixer, whisk the egg and sugar together until light and fluffy. Add the milk, flour and butter and whisk briefly until the batter is smooth.

Pour the batter evenly into the tin, smooth out and bake for 15–20 minutes, or until golden brown.

Leave to stand in the tin for 5 minutes, then turn out and place, right side up, on a wire rack to cool.

To make the filling

Meanwhile, cut the rhubarb stalks into 2 cm (¾ inch) pieces.

Place in a baking dish with 60 ml (2 fl oz) water and sprinkle with the sugar.

Roast in the oven for 10 minutes, or until the rhubarb is just tender. Set aside to cool.

Dissolve the jelly crystals in boiling water and then leave until cool and just beginning to set.

To assemble

Place the rhubarb pieces decoratively in the recess of the cooked and cooled flan.

Spoon the partially set jelly on top and leave to set completely.

Serve with the whipped cream.

Apple Lemon Delicious Pudding

SERVES 6

2 granny smith apples

60 g (2¼ oz) softened salted butter

170 g (6 oz) white (granulated) sugar

3 eggs, separated

70 g (2½ oz) self-raising flour

80 ml (2½ fl oz) milk

60 ml (2 fl oz) lemon juice

3 teaspoons finely grated lemon zest

125 ml (4 fl oz) pouring cream, to serve

This luscious pudding is a twist on the old-fashioned favourite, lemon delicious.

A layer of apple slices lifts the dessert to a whole new level, settling into three layers that mix and meld together. This dessert is truly memorable for all those who love lemon and/or custard.

~~~~~~~~

Preheat the oven to 150°C (300°F). Grease a 23 cm (9 inch) cast-iron frying pan or round baking dish, 8 cm (3¼ inches) deep.

Peel and core the apples and then cut into thin slices. Place decoratively over the base of the dish.

Using hand-held beaters or a stand mixer, whisk the butter, sugar and egg yolks together until well combined then, using a large metal spoon, fold in the flour, milk, lemon juice and zest.

Using hand-held beaters or a stand mixer, whisk the egg whites to stiff peaks, then fold into the batter until just combined.

Pour this on top of the apples and bake for 40 minutes, or until set.

Leave to stand for 5 minutes before serving with a jug of cream to share.

Apple Day

There are a number of apple orchards dotted around the Derwent Valley. In my opinion, the sight of an apple orchard in full fruit on a sunny, crisp, icy Valley morning is one of the best you could ever wish to see, all the more so when you've been invited to come and pick the gleanings.

This has come to be an annual pilgrimage. One day in early winter we pack our old ute with buckets and head to a secret location high in the hills of the Valley. It's an idyllic spot with sweeping views of the Derwent River and its surrounding hills and mountains. In the early morning bright sunshine with frosty grass crunching under our boots, we head down the rows of a large orchard.

By this stage, with the main harvest over, the birds are enjoying a feast of the apples remaining on the trees. However, they won't be deprived of their winter fodder as there are plenty of apples for all takers.

Before long the ute's tray is loaded to the brim. Its precious cargo is then secured and we head for home.

For about two weeks the apples sit in our shed, the sugars developing, waiting for the next stage – processing.

This is one of the most enjoyable times of the year. From the break of day, friends, neighbours and family begin arriving for the designated day of juicing.

Several work stations are set up in the shed in advance. First there's the apple washing. Next comes the area for the rough chopping of each piece of fruit so that they fit into the scratter (muncher), a device we've adapted from a (brand new) under-sink garbage disposal unit. The resulting pulp is transferred to a large Italian wine press to extract the juice. The wine press has a lovely history. It belonged to a friend (her Italian family had used it for generations), and she kindly gifted it to us, even arranging transport across Bass Strait. It's been joined since by a mini-me version, a gift from another friend in a neighbouring valley.

Every year I secretly wonder how those in the shed can be so happy at their work. It's icy cold in there and their hands must be near frozen from the cold water. I prefer to stay in the warmth of the kitchen and bake for them. Perhaps their good humour has something to do with the mugs of mulled cider with which I ply them – it's prepared and kept hot in large slow cookers.

They need to keep their strength and resilience levels high, so many snacks are baked, savoury and sweet, and a generous lunch, plus there's an endless supply of hot soup on the go.

The day is unfailingly productive. The amount of juice produced from such an informal operation is astounding. My husband, Robert, fills at least eight barrels for his cider, which is shared when it's ready months later with the friends and family that helped on the day.

Inside, I am eventually handed at least 20 litres (4¼ gallons) of the juice – this is poured into bottles and preserved.

Everyone goes home with at least 2 litres (70 fl oz) of the freshly pressed juice – a down payment of sorts for the cider to come.

The next day the spent pulp is given to the sheep and our pet pig Cilla. Any excess is sent to the neighbours for their various animals.

It's a day that demonstrates the strength and pleasure of the company of family and friends, where baking for them serves a really useful and productive purpose.

It is definitely one of my favourite days of the year.

Whisky & Orange Chocolate Self-Saucing Pudding

SERVES 4–6

FOR THE SPONGE

150 g (5½ oz) self-raising flour

pinch of sea salt

100 g (3½ oz) white (granulated) sugar

25 g (1 oz) cocoa

2 teaspoons finely grated orange zest

60 g (2¼ oz) salted butter, melted

125 ml (4 fl oz) milk

1 teaspoon vanilla extract

FOR THE SAUCE

100 g (3½ oz) soft brown sugar

20 g (¾ oz) cocoa

300 ml (10½ fl oz) boiling water

60 ml (2 fl oz) whisky

40 ml (1¼ fl oz) orange juice

While a chocolate self-saucing pudding is always a favourite, this recipe takes the concept to a whole new, supremely delicious, level.

To make the sponge

Preheat the oven to 170°C (325°F). Grease an 18–20 cm (7–8 inch) round baking dish, 10 cm (4 inches) deep.

Whisk together all the sponge ingredients until smooth.

Spoon this batter evenly into the dish.

To make the sauce

Sprinkle the combined brown sugar and cocoa over the sponge mixture.

In a separate bowl, mix together the boiling water, whisky and orange juice and pour carefully over the sponge mixture.

Bake for 30 minutes until the sponge has risen and is firm to the touch.

Rhubarb & Apple Pie

SERVES 6–8

1 egg white, whisked

FOR THE PASTRY

125 g (4½ oz) very soft
salted butter

125 g (4½ oz) white
(granulated) sugar

1 egg

170 g (6 oz) plain
(all-purpose) flour

50 g (1¾ oz) self-raising flour

30 g (1 oz) custard powder

FOR THE FILLING

300 g (10½ oz) 'eating' apples
(such as envy, pink lady or red
delicious), peeled, cored and
cut into 1 cm (½ inch) cubes

300 g (10½ oz) rhubarb stalks,
ends trimmed, cut into
1.5 cm (⅝ inch) pieces

60 g (2¼ oz) white
(granulated) sugar

1 tablespoon cornflour
(cornstarch) mixed to a paste
with 40 ml (1¼ fl oz) cold water

This recipe is a particular favourite of a neighbour of ours, who one day when visiting us, reminisced about a special pudding made for him by his grandmother when he was a child. I set about recreating it for him. He remembered that the pie had small tender chunks of apple – I use 'eating' apples (rather than cooking apples such as granny smiths) for this reason. He also recalled it was served with a lovely egg custard – not surprising since rhubarb and custard have long been cheerful companions. Instructions for making a creamy egg custard are provided opposite as an option if you have the time and inclination to make it.

~~~~~~~~

To make the pastry

Using a hand whisk, mix the butter and sugar until creamy, then whisk in the egg for 1 minute.

In a separate bowl, combine the flours and custard powder then, using a large metal spoon, fold into the butter mixture to make a soft dough. Wrap in plastic wrap and place in the fridge for at least 30 minutes to firm up before using.

To make the filling

Place the apple and rhubarb in a saucepan with 100 ml (3½ fl oz) water and the sugar. Bring to the boil, then reduce the heat and simmer until the rhubarb is tender and slightly broken down. Gradually stir in enough cornflour paste to reach a thick custard consistency. Set aside to cool.

To assemble for baking

Preheat the oven to 170°C (325°F). Grease a 20 cm (8 inch) pie plate or baking dish, 6 cm (2½ inches) deep.

Cut one-third from the pastry, cover and set aside. Roll the remaining pastry out on a lightly floured surface until large enough to fit the base of the prepared dish. Press the dough into the dish and brush with the whisked egg white to seal.

Spread the cooled fruit mixture on top.

Roll out the remaining portion of dough into a round large enough to cover the dish, then place this over the fruit. Crimp the edges together with your fingers or a fork to firmly seal. Prick the top in several places with a fork.

Bake for 30 minutes, or until the pastry is golden brown.

Leave to cool for 20 minutes before serving.

Creamy Vanilla Custard

**SERVES 6–8
AS AN ACCOMPANIMENT**

2 eggs

100 g (3½ oz) white
(granulated) sugar

2 teaspoons cornflour
(cornstarch) mixed to
a paste with 20 ml (½ fl oz) milk

2 teaspoons custard powder
mixed to a paste with
20 ml (½ fl oz) milk

300 ml (10½ fl oz) milk

50 ml (1½ fl oz) pouring cream

½ teaspoon vanilla extract

2 teaspoons lemon juice

**In this recipe, custard powder is used for its reliability, ensuring
stability of the custard, as well as adding a little extra colour
and flavour.**

Whisk together the eggs and sugar until well combined. Whisk in
the cornflour paste and custard powder paste.

Meanwhile, heat the milk and cream to boiling point in a large
saucepan.

Whisk ½ cup of the hot milk and cream into the egg mixture,
stirring constantly, then pour this mixture into the remaining milk
in the saucepan, whisking constantly.

Cook over low heat until the custard thickens. Do not boil. Stir in the
vanilla and lemon juice.

If you are not serving the custard immediately, place a piece of baking
paper on the surface to stop a skin forming.

Blackberry & Apple Crostata

SERVES 8

1 egg white, whisked

FOR THE FILLING

500 g (1 lb 2 oz) apples, peeled, cored and cut into 1 cm (½ inch) cubes

500 g (1 lb 2 oz) blackberries

90 g (3¼ oz) white (granulated) sugar, or to taste

3 teaspoons lemon juice

3 teaspoons cornflour (cornstarch) mixed to a paste with 40 ml (1¼ fl oz) cold water

FOR THE PASTRY

125 g (4½ oz) very soft salted butter

200 g (7 oz) white (granulated) sugar

2 eggs

300 g (10½ oz) plain (all-purpose) flour

150 g (5½ oz) self-raising flour

1 teaspoon bicarbonate of soda (baking soda)

The impending autumn is heralded in Tasmania with the first of the season's apples and an abundance of wild blackberries. Along country lanes people can be seen picking these wild growing treasures. With the worst of the summer heat gone, there's a delightful chill in the early morning air, which makes for pleasant foraging – well, it would, if it weren't for the prickles. I admire the tenacity and dedication of those who go to these lengths – my husband included, who has constructed a special ladder that lies across the top of the brambles so as to get to the best in the middle of the patch.

I much prefer to stay at home, waiting for him to return with the bounty. I then set to work to make jam and jelly, and most certainly a neighbourhood favourite, this blackberry and apple crostata.

~~~~~~~

To make the filling

Place the apple in a saucepan with 60 ml (2 fl oz) water, bring to the boil and then reduce the heat and simmer until the apple is just tender. Add the blackberries and bring to the boil again, then reduce the heat and simmer for 5 minutes. Stir in the sugar and lemon juice.

While still simmering, gradually stir in enough of the cornflour paste to reach a thick custard consistency.

Set aside to cool completely.

To make the pastry

Using a hand whisk, mix the butter and sugar until creamy, then whisk in the eggs for 1 minute. In a separate bowl, sift the dry ingredients together then, using a large metal spoon, fold into the egg mixture until well combined. Cover and set aside while waiting for the filling to cool.

To assemble for baking

Preheat the oven to 170°C (325°F). Grease a 25 x 30 cm (10 x 12 inch) slab tin, 6 cm (2½ inches) deep.

Cut one-third from the pastry and set aside. On a lightly floured surface, roll out the large piece of pastry to the size of the tin. Press the pastry evenly into the tin and then brush with some of the whisked egg white to seal. Spread the cooled fruit mixture over this.

Roll the remaining pastry out and cut into 8 mm (⅜ inch) strips (for a fancy edging, use a fluted pastry cutter if you have one). Place these in a lattice pattern over the top of the fruit.

Bake for 30 minutes, or until nicely browned.

Pear & Ginger Caramel Pudding

SERVES 4–6

FOR THE PUDDING

75 g (2¾ oz) plain
  (all-purpose) flour

75 g (2¾ oz) self-raising flour

2 teaspoons ground ginger

130 g (4½ oz) white
  (granulated) sugar

100 ml (3½ fl oz) coconut milk

1 egg

750 g (1 lb 10 oz) pears,
  peeled, cored and cut into
  1.5 cm (⅝ inch) pieces

60 g (2¼ oz) walnuts,
  roughly chopped

50 g (1¾ oz) glacé ginger,
  finely chopped

FOR THE CARAMEL

130 g (4½ oz) soft brown sugar

70 g (2½ oz) salted butter, melted

160 ml (5¼ fl oz) boiling water

3 teaspoons lemon juice

This dessert encapsulates several different flavours and textures. The pears combine so well with the caramel, which is contrasted and enhanced by the warmth of glacé ginger and the crunch of walnuts. Coconut milk is used for an interesting and delicious flavour.

~~~~~~

To make the pudding

Preheat the oven to 160°C (315°F). Grease a 20 cm (8 inch) round baking dish, 8 cm (3¼ inches) deep.

In a large bowl, mix together the flours, ground ginger and sugar.

In a separate bowl, whisk together the coconut milk and egg until well combined.

Make a well in the centre of the dry ingredients, then pour the egg mixture into this and mix with a metal spoon until smooth. Fold in the pear, along with the walnuts and glacé ginger.

Transfer to the dish and level out.

To make the caramel

In a heatproof bowl, combine the brown sugar, butter, boiling water and lemon juice and stir until the sugar dissolves.

Pour gently over the pudding batter.

Bake for 30 minutes, or until well risen and golden brown.

Simple Autumnal Strudel

SERVES 4–6

500 g (1 lb 2 oz) autumn fruits such as quinces, apples or pears, cut into 8 mm (⅜ inch) dice

1 sheet ready-rolled puff pastry, thawed

80 g (2¾ oz) white (granulated) sugar, plus 2 teaspoons extra

pinch of ground nutmeg, to taste (optional)

pinch of ground cloves, to taste (optional)

½ teaspoon ground cinnamon, to taste, plus ½ teaspoon extra

3 teaspoons custard powder or cornflour (cornstarch)

1 egg yolk whisked with 20 ml (½ fl oz) water, for glaze

This easy version of strudel was invented during our first COVID-19 lockdown, when even to go to the supermarket was a serious undertaking. It meant that I needed to bake with whatever I had at hand.

One day, in the absence of filo pastry, I simply rolled out a ready-rolled puff pastry sheet until it was very thin, and to my surprise it worked remarkably well.

~~~~~~~~

Preheat the oven to 200°C (400°F) and line a baking tray with baking paper.

If using quinces, steam the diced fruit for 3 minutes to soften a little, then set aside.

On a lightly floured surface, roll the pastry out very thinly into a large rectangle, about twice the size of the original sheet.

Mix the fruit, sugar, spices and custard powder together. Spoon in a mound along one-third of the pastry sheet, leaving a 5 cm (2 inch) strip clear on three sides and an 8 cm (3¼ inch) strip on the fourth.

Brush the edges of the pastry with a little of the egg wash, then fold over to enclose the filling so that it resembles a strudel shape. Press the edges together firmly.

Brush the top with the egg wash and sprinkle with the extra sugar and cinnamon.

Bake for 30 minutes, or until golden brown.

Leave to stand for 10 minutes before cutting into portions to serve.

Chocolate Cherry Coconut Shortcake

SERVES 12–16

300 g (10½ oz) cherry jam

FOR THE BASE

125 g (4½ oz) very soft salted butter

125 g (4½ oz) white (granulated) sugar

1 egg, lightly whisked

220 g (7¾ oz) self-raising flour

30 g (1 oz) cocoa

FOR THE TOPPING

3 egg whites

170 g (6 oz) white (granulated) sugar

100 g (3½ oz) desiccated coconut

Here a chocolate shortbread crust is topped with a layer of cherry jam and a lovely, light macaroon-style topping provides a delightful contrasting crunch.

Preheat the oven to 160°C (315°F). Grease a 25 x 35 cm (10 x 14 inch) slab tin, 5 cm (2 inches) deep, and line with baking paper.

To make the base

Using a hand whisk, mix the butter and sugar together until creamy, then whisk in the egg until well combined.

In a separate bowl, combine the dry ingredients, then fold into the butter mixture with a metal spoon to make a soft dough.

Press the dough evenly into the tin.

To make the topping

Using hand-held beaters or a stand mixer, whisk the egg whites until soft peaks form, then gradually whisk in the sugar until soft peaks form again. Using a large metal spoon, fold in the coconut until well combined.

To assemble

Spread the cherry jam over the shortbread base. Spoon the meringue topping over the jam and smooth with the back of a damp spoon.

Bake for 30 minutes, or until the topping is golden brown and the base is cooked through.

Cut and serve straight from the tin.

Lemon Coconut Pudding

SERVES 6–8

FOR THE PASTRY

90 g (3¼ oz) very soft
    salted butter

90 g (3¼ oz) white
    (granulated) sugar

1 egg

20 ml (½ fl oz) milk

190 g (6¾ oz) plain (all-purpose)
    flour

½ teaspoon baking powder

FOR THE FILLING

2 x 395 g (13¾ oz) tins sweetened
    condensed milk

250 ml (9 fl oz) lemon juice

2 teaspoons finely grated
    lemon zest

6 egg yolks

FOR THE TOPPING

3 egg whites

250 g (9 oz) caster (superfine) sugar

1 teaspoon cornflour (cornstarch)

1 teaspoon apple cider vinegar

30 ml (1 fl oz) boiling water

125 g (4½ oz) desiccated coconut

50 g (1¾ oz) flaked almonds

This dessert is made up of three layers: a crisp shortcrust pastry, a supremely tasty lemon filling and a coconut meringue-like crust, topped with flaked almonds. Condensed milk – that old-fashioned yet still popular pantry staple – is included in this recipe for its unctuous sweetness, which is balanced by the generous amount of lemon juice.

To make the pastry

Preheat the oven to 170°C (325°F). Grease a 22 x 30 cm (8½ x 12 inch) slab tin, 6 cm (2½ inches) deep.

Using a hand whisk, mix the butter and sugar together until creamy, then whisk in the egg and milk.

In a separate bowl, combine the dry ingredients then, using a large metal spoon, fold into the butter mixture until well combined. Wrap in plastic wrap and place in the fridge for at least 30 minutes to firm up before using.

On a lightly floured surface, roll out the pastry to around 5 mm (¼ inch) thick. Press into the base of the tin. Prick the pastry in several places with a fork. Bake for 15 minutes, or until light golden brown.

Remove from the oven and allow to cool.

To make the filling

Whisk together the condensed milk, lemon juice, zest and egg yolks until well combined and smooth. Pour this into the cooled pastry case.

Return to the oven, reduce the temperature to 150°C (300°F) and bake for 15 minutes.

Remove from the oven and reduce the oven temperature to 130°C (250°F).

To make the topping

Place the egg whites, sugar, cornflour and vinegar in a heatproof bowl, then pour in the boiling water. Using hand-held beaters or a stand mixer, beat until stiff peaks form. Using a large metal spoon, fold in the coconut.

Spread the mixture evenly over the set lemon filling, then gently press the flaked almonds into the surface.

Return to the oven and bake for 25–30 minutes, or until the coconut meringue layer is crisp on the outside and still a little like marshmallow in the centre.

Leave to stand for 20 minutes before cutting into squares to serve.

Cherry Tart

SERVES 6

FOR THE PASTRY

125 g (4½ oz) very soft salted butter

80 g (2¾ oz) white (granulated) sugar

1 teaspoon finely grated lemon zest

1 egg

100 g (3½ oz) plain (all-purpose) flour

80 g (2¾ oz) self-raising flour

FOR THE FILLING

1 x 680 g (1 lb 8 oz) jar sour (Morello) cherries, drained, or 400 g (14 oz) pitted fresh cherries (see Note)

60 g (2¼ oz) white (granulated) sugar

3 teaspoons cornflour (cornstarch) mixed to a paste with 40 ml (1¼ fl oz) cold water

This recipe is bursting with the tang of cherries, matched to an easy buttery pastry that is infused with the flavour of fresh lemon.

To make the pastry

Preheat the oven to 190°C (375°F). Grease a 20 cm (8 inch) tart plate, 3 cm (1¼ inches) deep.

Cream the butter, sugar and lemon zest together with a wooden spoon, then whisk in the egg until well combined.

In a separate bowl, combine the flours and, using a large metal spoon, fold into the butter mixture to form a soft dough.

Wrap in plastic wrap and refrigerate for 1 hour to firm up before using.

To make the filling

Place the cherries, sugar and 80 ml (2½ fl oz) water in a saucepan and bring to the boil. Reduce the heat and simmer for 5 minutes, then stir in enough of the cornflour paste to reach a thick consistency, cooking for 1 minute more.

Remove from the heat and allow to cool completely.

To assemble for baking

Cut one-third from the pastry, cover and set aside.

Roll out the remaining pastry on a lightly floured surface to fit the base and side of the tart plate. Crimp the edges decoratively with your fingers or a fork.

Spoon in the cooled filling.

Roll out the reserved pastry, cut into strips or desired shapes and place decoratively over the fruit.

Bake for approximately 30 minutes, or until the pie is golden brown.

Leave to stand for 20 minutes before serving.

NOTE *Sour cherries in jars, found on supermarket shelves, are called Morello cherries. When in season, fresh sweet varieties of cherries can be substituted for the sour cherries in this recipe. Kentish cherries, with their unique, delicious flavour are also a good option.*

Rustic Cherry Brandy Pie

SERVES 6

1 egg white, lightly whisked

FOR THE PASTRY

125 g (4½ oz) very soft
   salted butter

80 g (2¾ oz) white
   (granulated) sugar

1 egg

90 g (3¼ oz) plain
   (all-purpose) flour

90 g (3¼ oz) self-raising flour

FOR THE FILLING

1 x 680 g (1 lb 8 oz) jar sour
   (Morello) cherries, drained,
   or 400 g (14 oz) pitted fresh
   sour cherries

60 g (2¼ oz) white
   (granulated) sugar

2 teaspoons brandy

3 teaspoons cornflour (cornstarch)
   mixed to a paste with
   40 ml (1¼ fl oz) cold water

In this simple recipe, a sweet crisp, buttery crust is filled with the tangy goodness of sour cherries and a little brandy. It is delicious served with vanilla ice cream.

To make the pastry

Preheat the oven to 190°C (375°F). Grease a 20 cm (8 inch) round pie tin or tart plate, 4 cm (1½ inches) deep.

Using a hand whisk, mix the butter and sugar together, then whisk in the egg until well combined.

In a separate bowl, combine the flours and, using a large metal spoon, fold into the butter mixture to form a soft dough.

To make the filling

Place the cherries, sugar and 80 ml (2½ fl oz) water in a saucepan and bring to the boil. Reduce the heat and simmer for 5 minutes. Add the brandy, then gradually stir in enough cornflour paste to reach a thick custard consistency. Keep warm over low heat.

To assemble for baking

Cut one-third from the pastry, cover and set aside.

Press the remaining pastry evenly into the tin, then brush with some of the whisked egg white to seal.

Spoon in the warm cherry filling.

Break the reserved pastry dough into several pieces and flatten them between your (slightly damp) hands. Place them on top of the pie. Don't worry if they don't fit together – this will sort itself out during baking.

Bake for 25–30 minutes, or until golden brown. Leave to stand for at least 20 minutes before serving.

Chocolate Custard Cake with Glazed Peaches

SERVES 8

FOR THE CAKE

4 eggs

250 ml (9 fl oz) milk

380 g (13½ oz) white (granulated) sugar

50 g (1¾ oz) cocoa

1¼ teaspoons bicarbonate of soda (baking soda)

350 g (12 oz) self-raising flour

220 g (7¾ oz) salted butter, melted

30 ml (1 fl oz) apple cider vinegar

FOR THE CUSTARD

100 g (3½ oz) dark chocolate, chopped into small pieces

300 ml (10½ fl oz) milk

200 ml (7 fl oz) pouring cream

20 g (¾ oz) cocoa

60 g (2¼ oz) white (granulated) sugar

½ teaspoon vanilla extract

40 g (1½ oz) cornflour (cornstarch) mixed to a paste with 60 ml (2 fl oz) extra milk

FOR THE TOPPING

400 ml (14 fl oz) cream suitable for whipping

1 teaspoon icing (confectioners') sugar

½ teaspoon vanilla extract

825 g (1 lb 13 oz) tinned or preserved sliced peaches, drained, juice reserved

FOR THE GLAZE

170 g (6 oz) white (granulated) sugar

30 ml (1 fl oz) lemon juice

60 ml (2 fl oz) reserved peach juice

This dessert contains rich chocolate custard that fills a recess in a dark chocolate butter cake. Its crowning glory is a layer of whipped cream and sliced peaches finished with a lemon-infused glaze.

~~~~~~~

To make the cake

Preheat the oven to 160°C (315°F). Grease a 22 x 35 cm (8½ x 14 inch) baking dish, 7 cm (2¾ inches) deep. Line the base with baking paper, then grease again.

Using hand-held beaters or a stand mixer, beat all the cake ingredients for 3 minutes. Transfer to the dish.

Bake for 30 minutes, or until a metal skewer inserted into the centre comes out clean. Leave to stand in the tin for 5 minutes, before turning out onto a wire rack to cool completely.

To make the custard

Place the dark chocolate in a heatproof bowl. Heat the milk and cream with the cocoa, sugar and vanilla in a saucepan until boiling. Gradually stir in enough cornflour paste to reach a thick custard consistency. Remove from the heat and pour it over the chocolate. Cover the bowl for 2 minutes, then stir to melt the chocolate. Place a piece of baking paper on the surface to stop a skin forming. Set aside to cool.

To make the topping

Using hand-held beaters or a stand mixer, whip the cream, icing sugar and vanilla until soft peaks form. Pat the peach slices dry with paper towel.

To make the glaze

Place the sugar, lemon juice and the reserved peach juice in a small saucepan. Bring to the boil, stirring. Cook over medium heat, stirring occasionally, for 4–5 minutes, or until thickened slightly. Allow to cool.

To assemble

Place the cake on a serving platter. Cut a shallow recess in the cake, scooping out the crumb, and leaving a 1 cm (½ inch) rim around the outside.

Fill with the cooled chocolate custard and smooth it out. Spread with the whipped cream mixture. Place the peaches on top of the cream and then brush with the glaze.

Refrigerate for 30 minutes before serving.

NOTE *While tinned or preserved peaches are used in this dish, sliced fresh peaches could also be used. This cake will keep well in the fridge for up to 3 days.*

Peach, Lime & Raspberry Clafoutis with Lime Cream

SERVES 8–12

FOR THE CLAFOUTIS

3 eggs

250 g (9 oz) white (granulated) sugar

2 teaspoons finely grated lime zest

300 ml (10½ fl oz) milk

60 ml (2 fl oz) lime juice

20 g (¾ oz) natural or Greek-style yoghurt

400 g (14 oz) self-raising flour

40 g (1½ oz) plain (all-purpose) flour

125 ml (4 fl oz) light olive oil or vegetable oil

800 g (1 lb 12 oz) tinned or preserved sliced peaches, drained

200 g (7 oz) raspberries, fresh or frozen

FOR THE LIME CREAM

500 ml (17 fl oz) cream suitable for whipping

3 teaspoons icing (confectioners') sugar

70 g (2½ oz) natural or Greek-style yoghurt

2 teaspoons very finely grated lime zest

20 ml (½ fl oz) lime juice

In this clafoutis the flavour of lime subtly complements the peaches and raspberries.

It can be made several hours in advance and simply warmed in the oven for a few minutes before serving.

~~~~~~~~~~

To make the clafoutis

Preheat the oven to 160°C (315°F). Grease a 33 x 40 cm (13 x 16 inch) baking dish.

Using hand-held beaters or a stand mixer, whisk the eggs, sugar and lime zest together until creamy. Add the milk, lime juice, yoghurt, flours and oil and whisk until smooth.

Transfer to the dish and smooth out the surface. Place the peaches and raspberries decoratively over the top.

Bake for 20 minutes, or until golden brown.

To make the lime cream

Using hand-held beaters or a stand mixer, whip the cream and icing sugar together until soft peaks form. Add the yoghurt and whip again to soft-peak stage, then mix in the lime zest and juice.

Serve the lime cream alongside the clafoutis.

The lime cream can be prepared in advance and refrigerated for up to 2 days.

NOTE *While tinned or preserved peaches are used in this dish, sliced fresh peaches could also be used.*

Breads
& Buns

Making & Baking Yeasted Goods

In my opinion, there are few baking experiences more satisfying than that of baking bread.

In my later teenage years I lived with my nan, who was always so patient and tolerant of my fledgling efforts. I had no idea what I was doing really, but bought an entire 500 g (1 lb 2 oz) block of compressed yeast and worked my way through it, without much success.

I had buckets and bowls full of dough all over the house. There were lumps and smears of dough all over the benches, floor and even the walls. I tried making firm doughs and wet, nothing worked.

I suspect Nan's limitless patience came from the fact that her parents, my great-grandparents, owned a bakery in which she used to help when she was young.

After many months of continuing along these lines, I met a young woman who was an amazing cook, especially known for her expertise in baking bread. She gave me a few simple directions and in no time at all I was able to bake successful loaves.

That love of baking yeasted goods has never left me – I simply adore it.

With respect to shelf life, the type of bread determines how long it will keep. Breads with whole grains or dried fruit generally keep a little longer than the usual 2 to 3 days. It's best not to store bread in the fridge; this will toughen it and it will go stale faster. You can freeze bread for up to 3 months, but when thawed it will only be suitable for toasting. Bread is best stored at room temperature in a bread box. Alternatively, bread can be stored in a plastic bag or wrapped in foil, but this will soften the crust.

Rising times are approximate – they depend on the ambient temperature and humidity on any given day.

The recipes in this chapter are easily mastered with simple, readily accessible ingredients. I do tend to use a generous amount of yeast in most recipes, as I like to get results fairly quickly. Likewise with equipment – just your everyday mixing bowls and baking tins are required.

Once you get started and master the basics you can be as creative as you like. Bread is so accommodating and very forgiving.

Whatever you choose to bake, you can be guaranteed that your home will be filled with one of the most welcoming, enticing and appealing aromas of all.

Focaccia

SERVES 6–8

500 g (1 lb 2 oz) plain (all-purpose) flour

3 teaspoons instant dried yeast

1½ teaspoons sea salt

2 teaspoons white (granulated) sugar

2 garlic cloves, crushed (optional)

60 ml (2 fl oz) extra virgin olive oil, plus 100 ml (3½ fl oz) extra

375–400 ml (13–14 fl oz) warm water

2 tablespoons chopped rosemary and/or thyme

1½–2 teaspoons sea salt

This focaccia has a crisp crust and a soft, airy centre full of the flavour of olive oil, garlic and herbs. It is ideal for serving alongside robust, rustic casserole-style dishes, where it can be used to soak up flavoursome sauces. It is also perfect as an accompaniment to soups.

Mix the dry ingredients and garlic (if using) together in a large bowl. Make a well in the centre then, using a large metal spoon, stir in the 60 ml (2 fl oz) of oil and just enough of the warm water to make a soft dough, adding extra warm water if needed.

Cover the bowl with a clean tea towel and leave to rise until doubled in size – around 1 hour.

Turn out onto a lightly floured surface and knead for around 2 minutes, or until smooth, using extra flour if required.

Pour 50 ml (1½ fl oz) of the extra oil into a 25 x 35 cm (10 x 14 inch) slab (or lamington-style) tin, 5 cm (2 inches) deep, then pat out the dough to the same size as the tin and place inside the tin.

Preheat the oven to 210°C (410°F).

Allow the dough to rise in the tin for about 20 minutes until puffy, and then press your fingers into it at 1 cm (½ inch) intervals to make small impressions. Drizzle with the remaining oil and, finally, sprinkle over the herbs and sea salt.

Bake for 20–25 minutes, or until golden brown.

Remove from the oven, then allow to stand in the tin for 5 minutes before cutting into portions to serve.

NOTE *If the entire focaccia is not being used immediately, turn it out onto a wire rack at this point to ensure that it stays crisp as it cools.*

SERVES 4–6

1 egg yolk whisked with
20 ml (½ fl oz) water, for glaze

30 g (1 oz) grated tasty
cheese or 3 teaspoons
sesame seeds, for sprinkling

FOR THE DOUGH

300 g (10½ oz) plain
(all-purpose) flour

2 teaspoons instant
dried yeast

1 teaspoon white
(granulated) sugar

1 teaspoon sea salt

30 ml (1 fl oz) extra virgin olive oil

125 ml (4 fl oz) warm milk

125 ml (4 fl oz) warm water

FOR THE SPICED POTATO FILLING

400 g (14 oz) potatoes

20 ml (½ fl oz) extra virgin olive oil

2 teaspoons salted butter

150 g (5½ oz) onion, diced

1 garlic clove, crushed

1½ teaspoons ground cumin

1½ teaspoons paprika

½ teaspoon ground cardamom

½ teaspoon ground coriander

¼ teaspoon ground fennel

½ teaspoon dried oregano

¼ teaspoon chilli flakes

¼ teaspoon sumac

¼ teaspoon ground allspice

½ teaspoon soft brown sugar

20 g (¾ oz) tomato paste
(concentrated purée) mixed
with 40 ml (1¼ fl oz) water

80 g (2¾ oz) soft ricotta

Borek

This yeasted treat with a filling encased in ropes of dough is
a remarkable and delightful taste experience.

Two alternative fillings are provided here: spiced potato, and
cheese and spinach. Cut into wedges to serve, this is the perfect
accompaniment to soup although it can also be a stand-alone dish.
It's great for a picnic or school or work lunch boxes.

~~~~~~

To make the dough

Mix together the flour, yeast, sugar and salt in a large bowl. Make a well
in the centre then, using a large metal spoon, stir in the oil, milk and
enough water to make a soft dough.

Cover the bowl with a clean tea towel and leave to rise until doubled
in size – around 1 hour.

To make the potato filling

Wash the potatoes and bake or steam until just tender. Cool, and then
peel off the skins. Cut into 8 mm (⅜ inch) cubes and set aside.

Heat the oil and butter together over medium–low heat and sauté the
onion with the garlic until soft but not coloured.

Add the spices and cook for 1 minute more, stirring.

Transfer to a bowl and add the sugar and tomato paste mixture. Fold
in the cooked potato and ricotta, stirring gently to coat with the spices;
it doesn't matter if the potato breaks down a bit more. Season to taste.

To make the cheese and spinach filling

Cut the spinach, kale or silverbeet leaves into 6 mm (¼ inch) slices. Place
in a heatproof bowl. Pour boiling water over to just cover, then leave
to stand for 1 minute before draining in a colander and leaving to cool.
Place on paper towel and squeeze out any excess liquid.

In a large bowl, combine the blanched leaves with the remaining filling
ingredients and mix together until smooth. Season to taste.

To assemble for baking

Grease a 23 cm (9 inch) round cake tin, 8 cm (3¼ inches) deep. Line
the base with baking paper and grease again.

Turn the dough out onto a lightly floured surface and knead for
4 minutes, using extra flour if required. Dust a little more flour on the
bench, then roll the dough out to a rectangle 15 x 70 cm (6 x 27½ inches).

recipe continued overleaf

Borek . . . cont'd

**FOR THE CHEESE &
SPINACH FILLING**

100 g (3½ oz) spinach,
 kale or silverbeet (Swiss chard),
 tough stalks removed

boiling water

1 small onion, grated,
 or 2 spring onions (scallions),
 finely chopped

1 garlic clove, crushed

60 g (2¼ oz) soft ricotta

60 g (2¼ oz) Greek-style feta,
 crumbled

60 g (2¼ oz) tasty cheese,
 grated

30 g (1 oz) parmesan,
 finely grated

2 teaspoons chopped
 flat-leaf parsley

2 teaspoons chopped
 lemon thyme or
 regular thyme leaves

40 g (1½ oz) fresh
 breadcrumbs

¼ teaspoon sumac

2 teaspoons plain
 (all-purpose) flour

1 egg, lightly whisked

Dampen one long edge and each end with water. Place the selected filling along the dry long edge, fold the ends in and then roll, Swiss roll-style, to enclose the filling completely. You will now have a long rope shape.

Starting at one end, coil the rope around itself and then carefully place it in the tin. Cover with a clean tea towel and leave to rise for 25 minutes.

Preheat the oven to 200°C (400°F).

Use a damp finger to push an indent in the centre of the dough right through to the base – this will prevent the borek rising in the middle. Brush the top with some of the whisked egg mixture and sprinkle with either the tasty cheese or sesame seeds.

Bake for 10 minutes, then reduce the oven temperature to 170°C (325°F) and bake for 30 minutes more, or until golden brown and crisp.

Remove from the oven and leave to stand for 5 minutes before turning out onto a wire rack so that the base doesn't become soggy.

Serve warm or hot, cut into wedges or slices.

NOTE *Borek is delicious the next day, sliced and toasted in a sandwich press or on the grill.*

Everyday Bread
(recipe on page 146)

Family Pizza Slice

SERVES 4

250 g (9 oz) selected cheeses, such as mozzarella, grated tasty cheddar, grated parmesan, soft ricotta, feta

FOR THE DOUGH

350 g (12 oz) plain (all-purpose) flour

2 teaspoons instant dried yeast

1½ teaspoons sea salt

1 teaspoon white (granulated) sugar

20 ml (½ fl oz) extra virgin olive oil

260 ml (9 fl oz) warm water

FOR THE SAUCE

20 ml (½ fl oz) extra virgin olive oil

2 garlic cloves, crushed

1¼ teaspoons tomato paste (concentrated purée)

400 g (14 oz) tin diced tomatoes or fresh diced tomatoes

¾ teaspoon soft brown sugar

½ teaspoon sea salt

2 teaspoons tomato chutney

2 teaspoons worcestershire sauce

TOPPINGS OF YOUR CHOICE

e.g. salami, ham, cooked meats or seafood, semi-dried tomatoes, capsicum (pepper), onion, fresh herbs, anchovies

NOTE *It's important not to overload the pizza with toppings, as the base may not cook properly and it might become soggy.*

This is an easy way to prepare a pizza that will keep everyone in the family happy. The dough base is spread with a rich homemade tomato sauce – however, a purchased pizza sauce or passata could be used for the sake of convenience.

A selection of toppings can be placed on this base in strips according to personal tastes.

For a family of four the amount in this recipe is ideal. Simply double the recipe for a larger family.

To make the dough

Mix the dry ingredients together in a large bowl. Make a well in the centre then, using a large metal spoon, stir in the oil and enough of the warm water to make a soft dough. Don't add more water than is necessary or it will become too wet.

Cover the bowl with a clean tea towel and leave to rise until doubled in size – around 1 hour.

While the dough is rising, prepare the sauce.

To make the sauce

Heat the oil in a saucepan and sauté the garlic for 1 minute. Stir in the tomato paste and cook for 1 minute more. Add the remaining ingredients, then bring to the boil, stirring now and then. Reduce the heat to medium–low and simmer until thick. Remove from the heat and set aside to cool.

To assemble for baking

Preheat the oven to 210°C (410°F). Brush a 25 x 35 cm (10 x 14 inch) slab tin, 5 cm (2 inches) deep, liberally with olive oil.

Turn the dough out onto a lightly floured surface and knead for 2 minutes, or until smooth, using extra flour if required. Pat it out to the same size as the tin, then press it into place.

Spread the tomato sauce over the pizza base. (Any excess will keep for up to 3 days in the fridge or 2 months in the freezer – it's an excellent flavouring for gravies or casserole-style dishes.)

Sprinkle with a small amount of cheese.

Add your desired toppings and the remaining cheese (add any fresh herbs after cooking).

Bake for 15–20 minutes, or until the cheese is golden brown and bubbling.

Everyday Bread

MAKES 1 LARGE LOAF

450 g (1 lb) plain
  (all-purpose) flour

150 g (5½ oz) wholemeal
  or spelt flour

2 teaspoons soft brown sugar

2 teaspoons sea salt

3 teaspoons instant dried yeast

2 teaspoons apple cider vinegar

50 ml (1½ fl oz) extra virgin
  olive oil

500 ml (17 fl oz) warm water

There is nothing more welcoming than the aroma of hot baked bread. Freshly baked, sliced and buttered, or used the next day for toast, it is one of the simplest pleasures in life.

Although commercial and artisan varieties abound, there is something soul-satisfying about the aroma of yeast, the preparation, kneading, shaping and baking of dough. The following recipe is simple to make. I always use a generous amount of yeast so that it rises quite quickly, which I consider to be highly desirable.

If you prefer a slower ferment, try my wholemeal treacle bread recipe on page 163.

In a large bowl, mix together the flours, sugar, salt and yeast. Make a well in the centre of the dry ingredients then, using a large metal spoon, stir in the vinegar, oil and about three-quarters of the water. Mix to make a soft dough, adding extra warm water if needed.

Cover the bowl with a clean tea towel and leave to rise until doubled in size – around 1 hour.

Grease a 13 x 21 cm (5 x 8¼ inch) loaf tin, 8 cm (3¼ inches) deep.

Turn the dough out onto a lightly floured surface and knead for 5 minutes, or until smooth, using extra flour if required.

Cut the dough in half and shape each piece into a ball. Place the balls in the tin and leave to rise, covered loosely with a tea towel, for 20–30 minutes.

Preheat the oven to 200°C (400°F).

When the dough has risen to the top of the tin, bake for 40 minutes, or until the loaf is golden brown and sounds hollow when tapped.

Remove from the oven and transfer to a wire rack to cool.

NOTE *The inclusion of vinegar in this recipe helps to keep the bread fresh and improves the texture.*

Milk & Oat Bread

MAKES 1 LARGE LOAF

120 g (4¼ oz) rolled oats

180 ml (6 fl oz) warm milk

450 g (1 lb) plain
(all-purpose) flour

2 teaspoons sea salt

20 g (¾ oz) instant
dried yeast

40 ml (1¼ fl oz) extra virgin
olive oil

150 ml (5 fl oz) warm water,
plus extra if needed

This loaf is infused with the goodness and nutty flavour of rolled oats. It is further enriched with milk, which gives it a delightfully soft texture.

Place the oats in a saucepan and mix in the milk. Leave to stand for 30 minutes, then heat until lukewarm.

In a large bowl, mix together the flour, salt and yeast. Make a well in the centre of the dry ingredients then, using a large metal spoon, stir in the warm oat mixture, the oil and enough of the warm water to make a soft dough, adding extra warm water if needed.

Cover the bowl with a clean tea towel and leave to rise until doubled in size – around 1 hour.

Use a large spoon to turn the dough over, then leave to rise again, covered with a tea towel, for 30 minutes.

Grease a 13 x 21 cm (5 x 8¼ inch) loaf tin, 8 cm (3¼ inches) deep.

Turn the dough out onto a lightly floured surface and knead for around 5 minutes, or until smooth, using extra flour if required. Shape the dough into a loaf, place it in the tin and leave to rise, covered loosely with a tea towel, for 20–30 minutes.

Preheat the oven to 200°C (400°F).

When the dough has risen to the top of the tin, bake for 40 minutes, or until the loaf is golden brown and sounds hollow when tapped.

Remove from the oven and transfer to a wire rack to cool.

Multigrain Bread

MAKES 1 LARGE LOAF

100 g (3½ oz) grains,
such as rye, wheat,
malted barley or grits

300 g (10½ oz) plain
(all-purpose) flour

300 g (10½ oz) spelt flour

3 teaspoons instant
dried yeast

2 teaspoons sea salt

3 teaspoons soft
brown sugar

40 ml (1¼ fl oz) extra virgin
olive oil

375 ml (13 fl oz) warm water

Perhaps it is just my experience but sometimes when purchasing a wholegrain loaf, the seeds and wholegrains in it are almost impossible to chew and hard to digest. I have found that to alleviate this issue you simply need to cook the grain to a porridge first – soaking is not nearly enough in my opinion. After cooking, I blitz the mixture, but you can include the cooked grains whole if preferred. It's a matter of personal preference.

To cook the grains, place in a saucepan with 450 ml (16 fl oz) water over medium–high heat and bring to the boil. Reduce the heat and simmer for 30–40 minutes, or until the grain is tender. Process with a stick blender and add enough extra water to make a 'porridge' consistency. Blitz only briefly if you would like to retain some whole grains.

In a large bowl, mix together the flours, yeast, salt and sugar. Make a well in the centre of the dry ingredients then, using a large metal spoon, stir in the oil, 250 ml (9 fl oz) of the grain porridge and enough of the warm water to make a soft dough, adding extra warm water if needed.

Cover the bowl with a clean tea towel and leave to rise until doubled in size – around 1 hour.

Use a large spoon to turn the dough over, then leave to rise again covered with a tea towel, for 30 minutes.

Grease a 13 x 21 cm (5 x 8¼ inch) loaf tin, 8 cm (3¼ inches) deep.

Turn the dough out onto a lightly floured surface and knead for 5 minutes, or until smooth, using extra flour if required. Shape the dough into a loaf, place it in the tin and leave to rise, covered loosely with a tea towel, for 20–30 minutes.

Preheat the oven to 200°C (400°F).

When the dough has risen to the top of the tin, bake for 45 minutes, or until the loaf is golden brown and sounds hollow when tapped.

Remove from the oven and transfer to a wire rack to cool.

NOTE *It is quite likely that you will have some of the grain porridge left over. Simply refrigerate for 2 days or freeze in small 250 ml (9 fl oz) containers for 2 months.*

Cottage Cheese Bread

SERVES 6–8

450 g (1 lb) plain
(all-purpose) flour,
plus 30 g (1 oz) extra

2 teaspoons sea salt

1 teaspoon white
(granulated) sugar

3 teaspoons instant
dried yeast

1 tablespoon chopped
rosemary leaves or
¼ teaspoon dried rosemary

230 ml (7¾ fl oz) warm water

200 g (7 oz) creamed
cottage cheese

120 g (4¼ oz) pitted kalamata
olives, sliced

3 teaspoons (½ fl oz) milk,
for glaze

60 g (2¼ oz) parmesan,
finely grated

This is one of the most delicious breads you could ever wish to taste, and very simple to make.

The recipe yields two loaves, filled with olives and fresh rosemary and finished with a small amount of parmesan. It is wonderful served with soup or cheeses and pickles – but my favourite way of all is fresh from the oven, spread with lashings of softened butter.

Line a 30 x 35 cm (12 x 14 inch) baking tray with baking paper.

In a large bowl, mix together the flour, salt, sugar, yeast and rosemary. Set aside.

Place 125 ml (4 fl oz) of the warm water and the cottage cheese in a saucepan and stir over low heat until lukewarm.

Make a well in the centre of the dry ingredients then, using a large metal spoon, stir in the cottage-cheese mixture along with enough of the remaining water to make a soft dough. Cover the bowl with a clean tea towel and leave to rise until doubled in size – around 1 hour.

Meanwhile, pat the olives dry with paper towel or a clean cloth.

In a small bowl, gently mix the olives with 20 g (¾ oz) of the extra flour until combined.

When the dough has risen, use a large metal spoon to stir the olives through. Turn the dough out onto a lightly floured surface and knead for 3 minutes, or until smooth, using extra flour if required.

Cut the dough in half, then sprinkle each portion with the remaining extra flour. Shape each portion into a loaf 25 cm (10 inches) long. Place on the prepared tray and leave to rise, covered loosely with a tea towel, for 20 minutes.

Meanwhile, preheat the oven to 200°C (400°F).

Brush the loaves with a little milk and sprinkle with the parmesan. Bake for 20–25 minutes, or until the loaves are golden brown and sound hollow when tapped.

Remove from the oven and transfer to a wire rack to cool.

Savoury Pull-Apart Loaf

MAKES 1 LARGE LOAF

150 g (5½ oz) tasty cheese, grated

FOR THE DOUGH

450 g (1 lb) plain (all-purpose) flour

1 teaspoon white (granulated) sugar

1½ teaspoons sea salt

3½ teaspoons instant dried yeast

50 ml (1½ fl oz) extra virgin olive oil

350 ml (12 fl oz) warm water

FOR THE FILLING

50 g (1¾ oz) tomato paste (concentrated purée)

2 teaspoons tomato chutney

½ teaspoon sea salt

60 g (2¼ oz) salami or pepperoni, sliced

50 g (1¾ oz) semi-dried tomatoes

40 g (1½ oz) red or green capsicum (pepper), chopped

40 g (1½ oz) pitted kalamata olives, sliced

2 tablespoons chopped herbs such as rosemary, oregano or basil

This loaf is fun to make and delicious to eat. By its very nature it can be pulled apart – but it's also wonderful cut into slices, and this should only be done once the loaf has cooled completely. Serve it with soup or dishes with a gravy component.

The day after baking, any leftovers can be turned into French toast for a hearty breakfast or lunch.

~~~~~~~~

To make the dough

In a large bowl, mix together the flour, sugar, salt and yeast. Make a well in the centre then, using a large metal spoon, stir in the oil and enough warm water to make a soft dough, adding extra warm water if needed. Cover the bowl with a clean tea towel and leave to rise until doubled in size – around 1 hour.

Grease a 13 x 21 cm (5 x 8¼ inch) loaf tin, 10 cm (4 inches) deep. Line the base with baking paper, then grease again.

Turn the dough out onto a lightly floured surface and knead for around 5 minutes, or until smooth, using extra flour if required.

Roll the dough out to a rectangle 25 x 35 cm (10 x 14 inch), 1 cm (½ inch) thick.

To make the filling

Mix the tomato paste, chutney and 40 ml (1¼ fl oz) water in a small bowl and stir until well combined. Spread this over the dough.

To assemble

Scatter the remaining fillings on the dough, then sprinkle with 80 g (2¾ oz) of the grated cheese.

Roll up from the longer edge, Swiss roll-style, then cut into 7 cm (2¾ inch) pieces.

Place these randomly in the tin, at any angle. Press the top down a little so that the surface is more or less level. Sprinkle over the remaining cheese.

Cover the tin loosely with a clean tea towel and leave to rise for around 30 minutes – the dough should reach the top of the tin.

Meanwhile, preheat the oven to 200°C (400°F).

Bake for 15 minutes, then reduce the oven temperature to 180°C (350°F) and bake for 30 minutes more, or until dark golden brown.

Remove from the oven and leave to stand for 5 minutes, before running a knife around the edge and turning out onto a wire rack to cool.

The Motley Menagerie

Here in Tasmania during our first COVID-19 lockdown we became increasingly aware of the companionship value of the animals who live with us. The interactions between them – mostly good – were endlessly interesting.

This motley feather-and-fur crew consists of those that belonged to other people who could no longer care for them, or that had been suffering or neglected, and others who just needed a home.

Everyone's favourite is Cilla the pig, who had been bullied out of food by a larger pig in the enclosure at her former home. Her owner sent her here to see if we could fatten her up a bit. We fell in love with her sweet, gentle nature and obvious intelligence, so much so that he eventually allowed us to keep her as our pet. She is an absolute delight and has gone from being barely able to stand to now being fat and content.

When the cooking school closed temporarily due to COVID-19, she became noticeably depressed, missing the attention from the usual parade of admirers who attended the classes here.

We took to reading to her to cheer her up . . . after all, extended conversation with a pig is a bit challenging. We discovered she particularly liked Dr Seuss (although we spared her *Green Eggs and Ham*).

This situation drew the attention of a local radio station who ran a piece about pets coping during isolation.

Other great characters are the three geese. By most people's standards they are really quite revolting – noisy, aggressive, cantankerous. (They certainly fit the description.) However, they adore Cilla and are very protective of her.

They attack the sheep, but Anton the ram simply puts his massive head down and they bite his horns in spite. He thinks it's a rather nice massage so everyone is happy.

Old Tom, a feral cat who lived on the property when we came here and was eventually tamed, is ruler over the other cats and dog, who sense when he's in a bad mood and give him a wide berth, for fear of a swipe from his hook claw.

The Muscovy ducks, Millie, Molly and Mandy, are gentle creatures, though they rarely, if ever, lay an egg. They wander around the yard together, appearing to gossip among themselves.

The chickens, on the other hand, provide an abundance of eggs with which I can bake to my heart's content. The hens are happy as they free-range in the paddocks all day. Roosters have a bad reputation, I know. However, our Brewster the Rooster is a gentleman of the first order – he finds treats of worms and insects for his girls, calling them over so they can enjoy them first.

Poppy Puppy, our tiny Maltese Shih Tzu dog, tries her hand at rounding up the sheep. She is very brave about it until they step in her direction, which sends her scuttling back behind the protection of a gate.

Doris, the very old ewe, has long been toothless and would long ago have died were it not for a special treat she enjoys each morning. Last thing before bed my husband, Robert, fills two slow cookers with barley and water, which cooks to a porridge overnight ready for Cilla's breakfast. Doris gets a share fed to her off a large spoon, along with slivers of fresh apple. She may be old and arguably ugly now, but Anton the ram fell in love with her at first sight when he arrived here two years ago, and remains very protective of her to this day.

It's an idyllic lifestyle, we couldn't wish for better companionship. They ask for little in return, just the assurance of adequate food and shelter and no risk of impending harm.

We feel privileged to share their company.

Barmbrack (Irish Fruit Bread)

MAKES 2 ROUND LOAVES

130 g (4½ oz) raisins

100 g (3½ oz) currants

2 teaspoons sultanas

200 ml (7 fl oz) hot, strong black tea

60 ml (2 fl oz) whisky

550 g (1 lb 4 oz) plain (all-purpose) flour, plus 25 g (1 oz) extra

2 teaspoons ground cinnamon

1 teaspoon mixed spice

½ teaspoon ground nutmeg

½ teaspoon ground ginger

2 teaspoons finely grated lemon zest

70 g (2½ oz) soft brown sugar

2 teaspoons sea salt

4 teaspoons instant dried yeast

1 egg, lightly whisked

60 g (2¼ oz) salted butter, melted

200 ml (7 fl oz) warm milk

½ lightly whisked egg mixed with 20 ml (½ fl oz) whisky, for glaze

This Irish fruit bread is very special. Barmbrack means 'speckled loaf' and, indeed, this loaf fits the description, with a generous amount of raisins, currants and sultanas. In this recipe, the traditional soaking of the fruit in strong tea is taken a step further by introducing whisky to the equation, so that the loaf is lifted to a whole new dimension. Before baking, the egg glaze is enriched with a little more whisky.

Barmbrack can be sliced and served warm or cold spread with butter and is absolutely delicious toasted the next day.

~~~~~~~

In a heatproof bowl, mix together the dried fruit, hot tea and whisky and leave to stand for 1 hour.

Place a strainer over a small bowl and pour the fruit mixture into this, reserving the drained fruit and the soaking liquid.

In a large bowl, mix together the flour, spices, zest, sugar, salt and yeast.

In a separate bowl, using a hand whisk, mix the egg, butter, 100 ml (3½ fl oz) of the warm milk and the reserved soaking liquid.

Make a well in the centre of the dry ingredients then, using a large metal spoon, stir in the egg mixture, along with enough of the remaining warm milk to make a soft dough. Cover the bowl with a clean tea towel and leave to rise until doubled in size – around 1 hour.

Line two 30 x 35 cm (12 x 14 inch) baking trays with baking paper.

Turn the drained fruit out onto paper towel and press lightly to remove any excess liquid. Transfer to a bowl, then mix the fruit with the extra 25 g (1 oz) of flour with a large metal spoon to combine. Pour the fruit onto the risen dough and mix well to combine.

Turn the dough out onto a lightly floured surface and knead for around 3 minutes, or until smooth, using extra flour if required.

Cut the dough in half, sprinkle each portion with flour, then knead for 3 minutes. Shape each portion into an 18 cm (7 inch) round. Place on the trays and leave to rise, loosely covered with a clean tea towel, for 30 minutes.

Preheat the oven to 200°C (400°F).

Brush the loaves with the egg whisky glaze. Bake for 10 minutes, then reduce the oven temperature to 160°C (315°F) and bake for 20 minutes more, or until they sound hollow when tapped.

Remove from the oven and transfer to a wire rack to cool.

Cheese, Bacon & Thyme Twist

SERVES 6–8

FOR THE DOUGH

500 g (1 lb 2 oz) plain (all-purpose) flour

2 teaspoons sea salt

2 teaspoons white (granulated) sugar

3½ teaspoons instant dried yeast

60 g (2¼ oz) tasty cheese, grated

2 teaspoons chopped thyme or ¼ teaspoon dried thyme

1 egg, lightly whisked

250 ml (9 fl oz) warm milk

1 garlic clove, crushed

60 ml (2 fl oz) extra virgin olive oil

60 ml (2 fl oz) warm water, plus extra if needed

15 g (½ oz) salted butter, melted

FOR THE FILLING

180 g (6½ oz) tasty cheese, grated

2 spring onions (scallions), finely chopped

2 teaspoons chopped thyme

200 g (7 oz) rindless bacon, diced

In this bread the bold flavours of cheese and bacon intermingle with the freshness of garden herbs. It is enhanced by an unusual twisting of ropes of dough so that every mouthful is an explosion of flavour. It's a great loaf to serve with soups but it's delicious enough to eat just on its own.

~~~~~~~

To make the dough

In a large bowl, mix together the flour, salt, sugar, yeast, cheese and thyme. Make a well in the centre then, using a large metal spoon, stir in the egg, milk, garlic, oil and enough warm water to make a soft dough, adding extra warm water if needed. Cover the bowl with a clean tea towel and leave to rise until doubled in size – around 1 hour.

To assemble for baking

Line a large baking tray with baking paper.

Turn the dough out onto a lightly floured surface and knead for 5 minutes, or until smooth, using extra flour if required.

Roll the dough out to a rectangle 25 x 45 cm (10 x 17¾ inches). Brush a little water along one of the longer edges. Brush the rest of the surface with the melted butter.

For the filling, sprinkle 120 g (4¼ oz) of the cheese over the rest of the dough, along with the spring onion, thyme and bacon.

Roll the dough up, Swiss roll-style, from the longer, dry edge. Press to seal the seam. With the seam side underneath, use a sharp knife to cut the dough in half lengthways. At one end, press the edges together to seal well, then twist the lengths of dough one over the other to form a long twist. Don't worry if this gets a bit messy – it comes together in the end. Shape into a ring and seal the join well with a little water.

Place carefully on the tray and sprinkle with the remaining cheese. Cover loosely with a tea towel and leave to rise for 20 minutes.

Preheat the oven to 200°C (400°F).

Bake for 10 minutes, then reduce the oven temperature to 180°C (350°F) and bake for 25 minutes more, or until golden brown.

Remove from the oven and transfer to a wire rack to cool.

Pesto Finger Buns

MAKES 12

450 g (1 lb) plain
(all-purpose) flour

3 teaspoons instant
dried yeast

1 teaspoon white
(granulated) sugar

1½ teaspoons sea salt

3 teaspoons extra virgin
olive oil

300 ml (10½ fl oz) warm water

1 egg yolk whisked with
20 ml (½ fl oz) water, for glaze

200 g (7 oz) basil pesto

40 g (1½ oz) sesame seeds

These lovely buns sprinkled with crunchy sesame seeds hide a tangy pesto filling. They are perfect for serving as an accompaniment to soup or a pasta dish.

~~~~~~~~

Place the flour, yeast, sugar and salt in a large bowl and mix well. Make a well in the centre then, using a large metal spoon, stir in the oil and enough warm water to make a soft dough, adding extra warm water if needed. Cover the bowl with a clean tea towel and leave to rise until doubled in size – around 1 hour.

Line a baking tray with baking paper.

Turn the dough out onto a lightly floured surface and knead for around 5 minutes, or until smooth, using extra flour if required.

Cut the dough into 12 equal pieces and knead each into a roll 12 cm (4½ inches) long. Press out to an oval shape and brush around the edges with a little of the egg wash.

Place 3 teaspoons of pesto in the centre of each and spread out to cover all except the dampened edges. Fold in half and seal the edges. Shape each bun into a log and place side by side, seam side down on the tray.

Preheat the oven to 200°C (400°F).

Cover the buns loosely with a tea towel and leave to rise for 15 minutes. Brush the buns gently with the egg wash and sprinkle on the sesame seeds.

Bake for around 15 minutes, or until well risen and golden.

Remove from the oven and transfer to a wire rack to cool.

Slow Ferment Wholemeal Treacle Bread

MAKES 1 LARGE LOAF

420 g (15 oz) plain
  (all-purpose) flour

180 g (6½ oz) wholemeal flour

2 teaspoons sea salt

¾ teaspoon instant dried yeast

90 g (3¼ oz) potato,
  finely grated

20 ml (½ fl oz) extra virgin
  olive oil

3 teaspoons treacle

400 ml (14 fl oz) warm water

This is a delicious loaf made in the tradition of long and luxurious rising. The grated potato in the mixture gives a lovely softness to the dough and improves its keeping quality.

In a large bowl, mix together the flours, salt and yeast, then stir in the grated potato using a large metal spoon. Make a well in the centre and pour in the oil.

In a separate bowl, use a hand whisk to dissolve the treacle in the warm water. Pour almost all of this liquid into the flour mixture and stir to make a soft dough, adding extra liquid if needed.

Cover the bowl with a tea towel and leave to rise until doubled in size – this could take upwards of six hours, even overnight.

Preheat the oven to 200°C (400°F). Grease a 13 x 21 cm (5 x 8¼ inch) loaf tin, 8 cm (3¼ inches) deep.

Turn the dough out onto a lightly floured surface and knead for 5 minutes, or until smooth, using extra flour if required. Shape the dough into a log and press into the tin. Cover the tin loosely with a clean tea towel and leave to rise for around 1 hour – the dough should reach the top of the tin.

Bake for 40 minutes, or until the loaf is golden brown and sounds hollow when tapped.

Remove from the oven and transfer to a wire rack to cool.

Coconut Custard & Passionfruit Ring

SERVES 6

1 egg yolk whisked with
   20 ml (½ fl oz) water,
   for glaze

FOR THE COCONUT CUSTARD

400 ml (14 fl oz) coconut milk

40 g (1½ oz) custard powder

25 g (1 oz) white (granulated) sugar

3 teaspoons lemon juice

FOR THE DOUGH

350 g (12 oz) plain
   (all-purpose) flour

1½ teaspoons sea salt

15 g (½ oz) white
   (granulated) sugar

3½ teaspoons instant
   dried yeast

125 ml (4 fl oz) warm milk

60 g (2¼ oz) salted butter,
   melted

1 egg, lightly whisked

120 ml (4 fl oz) warm water

FOR THE DRIZZLE

300 g (10½ oz) icing
   (confectioners') sugar,
   sifted

1 teaspoon salted butter,
   melted

pulp of 1–2 passionfruit

3 teaspoons lemon juice

These semisweet luscious buns are filled with coconut milk custard and topped with tangy passionfruit drizzle.

~~~~~~~~

To make the coconut custard

Place 300 ml (10½ fl oz) of the coconut milk in a saucepan over medium heat and bring to the boil.

Meanwhile, in a small bowl, whisk together the remaining coconut milk and the custard powder to make a thin paste. When the milk has reached boiling point, whisk in the custard powder paste until thickened. Stir in the sugar and then the lemon juice. Remove from the heat and place a piece of baking paper on the surface to stop a skin forming. Set aside to cool completely.

To make the dough

In a large bowl, mix together the flour, salt, sugar and yeast. Make a well in the centre then, using a large metal spoon, stir in the milk, melted butter, egg and enough warm water to make a soft dough. Cover the bowl with a clean tea towel and leave to rise until doubled in size – around 1 hour.

To assemble for baking

Preheat the oven to 200°C (400°F). Grease a 20 cm (8 inch) ring tin, 6 cm (2½ inches) deep. Line the base with baking paper and grease again.

Turn the dough out onto a lightly floured surface and knead for 5 minutes, or until smooth, using extra flour if required. Cut the dough into six equal portions and shape each into a ball. Flatten each ball to form a 15 cm (6 inch) diameter circle and brush with the egg glaze.

Spoon four generous teaspoons of the custard into the centre of each circle. Fold each circle in half to form a crescent shape, then use your fingers to crimp the edges together to seal and reshape into a ball. Place seam side down in the tin. Cover loosely with a tea towel and leave to rise for around 20 minutes.

Bake for 20 minutes, or until golden brown. Remove from the oven and leave to stand in the tin for 5 minutes. Turn out onto a wire rack. Leave to cool.

To make the drizzle

Use a metal spoon to mix together the sifted icing sugar, melted butter, passionfruit pulp and just enough of the lemon juice to make a smooth icing. Add a little hot water (a few drops at a time) if more liquid is needed to make a drizzling consistency. Spoon the drizzle over the top of the cooled buns, then leave for around 30 minutes to set. Pull the buns apart when you are ready to serve.

Coffee Scrolls

MAKES 9

FOR THE DOUGH

450 g (1 lb) plain (all-purpose) flour

3½ teaspoons instant dried yeast

30 g (1 oz) white (granulated) sugar

1½ teaspoons sea salt

1 egg, lightly whisked

45 g (1½ oz) very soft salted butter

150 ml (5 fl oz) warm espresso coffee

125 ml (4 fl oz) warm milk

FOR THE FILLING

60 g (2¼ oz) salted butter, melted

180 g (6½ oz) soft brown sugar

2 teaspoons instant coffee powder

2 teaspoons warm espresso coffee

90 g (3¼ oz) sultanas or other dried fruit

FOR THE DRIZZLE

220 g (7¾ oz) icing (confectioners') sugar

1 teaspoon salted butter, melted

40 ml (1¼ fl oz) espresso coffee, cooled

These scrolls resemble traditional Chelsea buns, with a rich coffee filling. A drizzle of espresso icing over the top completes these delectable sweet treats.

It may seem a little unusual to include instant coffee powder and espresso in the same recipe, but this is absolutely the best way to achieve the ultimate coffee flavour in these scrumptious buns.

To make the dough

In a large bowl, combine the flour, yeast, sugar and salt. Make a well in the centre then, using a large metal spoon, stir in the egg, butter, espresso and enough of the milk to make a soft dough.

Cover the bowl with a clean tea towel and leave to rise until doubled in size – around 1 hour.

To make the filling

Using a metal spoon, mix the filling ingredients together, except the sultanas, to make a soft spreadable consistency.

To prepare for baking

Grease a 20 cm (8 inch) square baking tin, 8 cm (3¼ inches) deep and line the base with baking paper. Grease again.

Turn the dough out onto a lightly floured surface and knead for 2 minutes, or until smooth, using extra flour if required. Roll the dough out to a rectangle 25 x 35 cm (10 x 14 inches). Use a spatula to spread the coffee filling over the dough, then sprinkle with the sultanas. Roll the dough up, Swiss roll-style, from the longer edge.

With a sharp knife, cut the roll into nine equal pieces. Turn the pieces cut-side up and place them in the tin, then cover loosely with a tea towel. Leave to rise for 20–30 minutes.

Preheat the oven to 200°C (400°F).

Bake for 5 minutes, then reduce the oven temperature to 180°C (350°F) and bake for 15 minutes more.

Remove from the oven and allow to rest in the tin for 5 minutes before turning out onto a wire rack to cool completely.

To make the drizzle

When the buns are cool, place the icing sugar and melted butter in a bowl and stir in enough of the espresso to make a drizzling consistency.

Spoon the icing over the buns and leave to set. Pull apart when you are ready to serve.

Walnut Twirl

SERVES 6–8

FOR THE DOUGH

450 g (1 lb) plain
  (all-purpose) flour

3 teaspoons instant
  dried yeast

2 teaspoons sea salt

40 g (1½ oz) soft brown sugar

2 eggs, lightly whisked

50 g (1¾ oz) salted butter,
  melted

220 ml (7½ fl oz) warm milk

FOR THE FILLING

300 g (10½ oz) finely
  ground walnuts

90 g (3¼ oz) soft brown sugar

45 g (1½ oz) fresh breadcrumbs

1 teaspoon mixed spice

1 teaspoon ground cinnamon

3¼ teaspoons cornflour
  (cornstarch)

1 teaspoon finely grated
  lemon zest

1 teaspoon finely
  grated orange zest

30 ml (1 fl oz) lemon juice

30 ml (1 fl oz) orange juice

20 ml (½ fl oz) milk

1 egg, whisked

FOR THE GLAZE

1 egg yolk whisked with
  20 ml (½ fl oz) water

1 teaspoon ground
  cinnamon

1 teaspoon white
  (granulated) sugar

Every bite of this delicious roll contains a creamy walnut filling bursting with a subtle hint of citrus.

To make the dough

In a large bowl, mix together the flour, yeast, salt and sugar. Make a well in the centre then, using a large metal spoon, stir in the eggs, melted butter and enough warm milk to make a soft dough. Cover the bowl with a clean tea towel and leave to rise until doubled in size – around 1 hour.

To make the filling

Place all the filling ingredients in a bowl and stir together to make a smooth paste, adding a little water if necessary to make a spreading consistency.

To assemble for baking

Line a 30 x 40 cm (12 x 16 inch) baking tray with baking paper.

Turn the dough out onto a lightly floured surface and knead for 4 minutes, or until smooth, using extra flour if required.

Roll out the dough to form a rectangle 30 x 45 cm (12 x 17¾ inches).

Cut the dough in half lengthways with a sharp knife. Brush an 8 mm (⅜ inch) wide strip of water along one long edge of both pieces.

Divide the filling in half, then use a spatula to spread it over each piece of dough. Roll each piece up, Swiss roll-style, from the dry edge to the wet and position the pieces side by side.

Dampen one end of each piece with water then twist the ends together. Make the twirl by placing (weaving) one log over the other to form a long spiral. Press each end together to form a log 40 cm (16 inches) long.

Place the log carefully on the tray (you may need to position it diagonally so that it fits). Cover loosely with a tea towel and leave to rise for 20 minutes.

Preheat the oven to 200°C (400°F).

Just before baking, brush the dough with the egg wash and sprinkle with the cinnamon and sugar.

Bake for 10 minutes, then reduce the oven temperature to 170°C (325°F) and bake for 30 minutes more.

Remove from the oven and allow to rest in the tin for 5 minutes before turning out onto a wire rack to cool completely.

Apricot & Cranberry Buns

MAKES 12

450 g (1 lb) plain
  (all-purpose) flour, plus
  25 g (1 oz) extra

3 teaspoons soft
  brown sugar

3 teaspoons finely
  grated lemon zest

3 teaspoons instant
  dried yeast

1½ teaspoons sea salt

1 egg, whisked, plus
  1 lightly whisked egg extra,
  for glaze

60 g (2¼ oz) salted butter,
  melted

250 ml (9 fl oz) warm milk,
  plus extra if needed

180 g (6½ oz) dried apricots,
  chopped

120 g (4¼ oz) dried cranberries

250 ml (9 fl oz) boiling water

These soft and lovely buns are filled with the appealing colour, flavour and texture of apricot and cranberry, with a little hint of lemon. They are delicious served warm from the oven, cut in half and spread with a generous amount of butter.

The milk and butter content of the dough helps them keep well until the next day, when they can be served cold or reheated to release their wonderful aroma once more.

In a large bowl, mix together the flour, sugar, zest, yeast and salt. Make a well in the centre then, using a large metal spoon, stir in the whisked egg, butter and enough warm milk to make a soft dough, adding a little extra warm milk if needed.

Cover the bowl with a clean tea towel and leave to rise until doubled in size – around 1 hour.

Meanwhile, in a heatproof bowl, combine the apricots and cranberries and cover with the boiling water. Leave to stand for 30 minutes, then drain well.

Turn the drained fruit out onto paper towel and press lightly to remove any excess liquid. Transfer to a bowl and use a large metal spoon to mix the fruit with the extra 25 g (1 oz) flour.

Grease a 25 x 35 cm (10 x 14 inch) baking tray or line with baking paper.

Mix the fruit into the dough with a metal spoon.

Turn the dough out onto a lightly floured surface and knead for 3 minutes to bring it together well, using extra flour if required.

Cut the dough into 12 equal pieces and roll each into a ball. Place the balls on the tray, cover loosely with a tea towel and leave to rise for 20 minutes.

Preheat the oven to 200°C (400°F).

Gently brush the dough with the egg glaze. Bake for 20 minutes, or until golden brown.

Remove from the oven and turn out onto a wire rack to cool.

Tear-and-Share Raspberry Caramel Buns

MAKES 16

FOR THE DOUGH

400 g (14 oz) plain
   (all-purpose) flour

2 teaspoons instant
   dried yeast

15 g (½ oz) soft brown sugar

1 teaspoon sea salt

200 ml (7 fl oz) lukewarm milk

15 g (½ oz) Greek-style yoghurt

2 eggs, lightly whisked

2 teaspoons lemon juice

½ teaspoon vanilla extract

50 g (1¾ oz) salted butter,
   melted

FOR THE FILLING

100 g (3½ oz) frozen raspberries

FOR THE COATING

180 g (6½ oz) salted butter

160 g (5¾ oz) soft brown sugar

2 teaspoons lemon juice

A delicious rich caramel provides the perfect contrast to the tang of the raspberries that fill these buns. As the caramel cools, it starts to set and makes a delicious crispy toffee on the outside of each bun. This helps to keep the buns fresh. While this dish can be baked in a round cake tin, it looks especially delightful when baked in a bundt tin or a tin with a decorative edge. Baker beware, however – that attractive pattern may cause the bun to stick in its grooves, so if you choose to go this way, be sure to grease the tin very well indeed.

~~~~~~~

To make the dough

In a large bowl, mix together the flour, yeast, brown sugar and salt.

In a separate bowl, whisk together the warm milk, yoghurt, eggs, lemon juice and vanilla.

Make a well in the centre of the dry ingredients then, using a large metal spoon, stir in the egg mixture and the melted butter to make a soft dough. Cover the bowl with a clean tea towel and leave to rise until doubled in size – around 1 hour.

Prepare either a 23 cm (9 inch) bundt tin, a 21 cm (8¼ inch) decoratively edged round tin or a 20 cm (8 inch) round cake tin. Whichever tin you use, it should be 10 cm (4 inches) deep. If using a round tin, grease well and line the base with baking paper. Grease again. If using a bundt or decorative tin, grease well.

Turn the dough out onto a lightly floured surface, dust with a little extra flour and knead for 3 minutes, or until smooth.

Cut the dough into 16 equal pieces and roll each into a ball. Pat each ball into a circle 8 mm (⅜ inch) thick. Brush the edge of half of each circle with a little water. Place 3 or 4 raspberries in the centre of each circle. Fold each circle in half to form a crescent shape, then use your fingers to crimp the edges together to seal and reshape into a ball.

To make the coating

Place the ingredients in a small saucepan and heat over medium–low heat, whisking until melted and well combined. Bring just to the boil, then immediately remove from the heat. Cool for 3 minutes.

Using two spoons, roll each dough ball very briefly in the caramel to coat, and then place seam side up in a circular pattern in the tin, layering as needed. If there is any caramel left, drizzle it over the top.

Cover with a tea towel and leave to rise for 20 minutes.

NOTE *Do not under any circumstances use a springform tin as the caramel will ooze out during baking.*

To bake

Preheat the oven to 190°C (375°F).

Bake the bun for 10 minutes, then reduce the oven temperature to 160°C (315°F) and bake for 25 minutes more if using a bundt tin, or 30 minutes if using a round tin. (The bun will brown quite quickly on top during baking, which is normal.) When cooked, the bun should sound hollow when tapped.

Leave to stand in the tin for 5 minutes before carefully inverting onto a platter.

To serve

Pull the buns apart with two forks to prevent the hot caramel burning your fingers.

Small
Savouries

~

Broccoli & Cauliflower Cheese Tarts

MAKES 8

2 sheets ready-rolled puff pastry, thawed, or 1 quantity of Easy Flaky Pastry (page 226)

80 g (2¾ oz) camembert

30 g (1 oz) parmesan, finely grated

FOR THE FILLING

150 g (5½ oz) cauliflower florets, cut into 4 cm (1½ inch) pieces

200 g (7 oz) broccoli florets, cut into 4 cm (1½ inch) pieces

25 g (1 oz) cornflour (cornstarch)

550 ml (19 fl oz) milk

1 egg yolk, lightly whisked

½ teaspoon dijon mustard

100 g (3½ oz) grated tasty cheese, plus 60 g (2¼ oz) extra

These creamy, tasty tarts have oozy bites of camembert in the centre and are encapsulated in crispy puff pastry. Served piping hot from the oven, they are bound to be a family favourite.

Ready-rolled pastry sheets are specified in this recipe for the sake of convenience, however, you could instead make a batch of Easy Flaky Pastry (see page 226) to add a luxurious dimension of golden brown crunchiness.

~~~~~~

To make the filling

Steam the cauliflower and broccoli separately until just tender.

In a small bowl, whisk together the cornflour and 50 ml (1½ fl oz) of the milk, then whisk in the egg yolk and mustard until smooth. Set aside.

In a large saucepan over medium heat, bring the remaining 500 ml (17 fl oz) of milk to a simmer, then gradually whisk in enough cornflour paste to reach a thick custard consistency.

Stir in the 100 g (3½ oz) of grated tasty cheese until melted and then fold in the broccoli and cauliflower. Remove from the heat and set aside to cool.

To assemble for baking

Preheat the oven to 200°C (400°F). Grease eight 200 ml (7 fl oz) pie tins.

Cut four 12 cm (4½ inch) circles from each pastry sheet, then press the pastry into the base and up the side of each pie tin.

Distribute the cooled filling mixture evenly between the tart cases.

Cut the camembert into eight cubes. Insert one in the centre of each tart.

Combine the 60 g (2¼ oz) of grated tasty cheese with the parmesan, then sprinkle this over the tarts.

Bake for 20–25 minutes, or until the pastry is crisp and golden and the topping is golden brown and bubbling. Leave in the tins for 5 minutes before serving, or transferring to a wire rack to cool.

NOTE *These tarts are excellent reheated the next day for a light lunch. This is best done in the oven at 150°C (300°F) for a few minutes.*

Ultimate Sausage Rolls

MAKES 20–24

2 ready-rolled puff pastry
 sheets, thawed

1 egg yolk whisked with
 20 ml (½ fl oz) water, for glaze

40 g (1½ oz) sesame seeds
 (optional)

FOR THE FILLING

250 g (9 oz) beef sausage mince

250 g (9 oz) beef mince

60 g (2¼ oz) soft ricotta

1 small onion, coarsely grated

40 g (1½ oz) carrot, finely grated

50 g (1¾ oz) celery,
 coarsely grated

1 garlic clove, crushed

2 teaspoons chutney

2 teaspoons soy sauce

3 teaspoons barbecue sauce

3 teaspoons tomato sauce
 (ketchup)

40 g (1½ oz) fresh breadcrumbs

½ teaspoon sea salt

There's so much to like about a good sausage roll – crisp and savoury served with a good tomato sauce or chutney. In this version the flavour and texture are enhanced by the addition of creamy ricotta along with the discreet inclusion of garden vegetables.

This recipe makes around two dozen small sausage rolls, although you could make them larger if desired.

~~~~~~~~~~

Preheat the oven to 200°C (400°F). Line two large baking trays with baking paper.

To make the filling

In a large bowl, use a large metal spoon or your hands to mix all the filling ingredients together, making sure that the mixture is very well combined. Set aside.

To assemble for baking

Cut each pastry sheet in half lengthways and brush down one long edge of each piece with some of the egg wash.

Divide the filling into four equal amounts. Use your hands to form each portion into a sausage shape long enough to fit the pieces of pastry, then place along the longer dry edge of each.

Roll up the pastry from the dry edge to the wet and seal, then position the rolls so that they are seam side down on the trays. Cut each long roll into 5 or 6 pieces. Prick each piece twice with a fork or the point of a sharp knife.

Brush with the egg wash and sprinkle on the sesame seeds (if using).

Bake for 15 minutes, or until puffed and golden brown.

Pork & Fennel Savoury Rolls

MAKES 12

2 ready-rolled puff
   pastry sheets, thawed

1 egg yolk whisked with
   20 ml (½ fl oz) water,
   for glaze

20 g (¾ oz) poppy seeds
   (optional)

FOR THE FILLING

20 ml (½ fl oz) extra virgin
   olive oil

120 g (4¼ oz) onion, diced

150 g (5½ oz) fennel, diced

1 garlic clove, crushed

70 g (2½ oz) rindless bacon,
   diced

500 g (1 lb 2 oz) pork mince

60 g (2¼ oz) creamed
   cottage cheese

80 g (2¾ oz) fresh
   breadcrumbs

40 g (1½ oz) celery,
   coarsely grated

50 g (1¾ oz) apple,
   coarsely grated

3 teaspoons chutney

2 teaspoons soy sauce

2 teaspoons barbecue sauce

1½ teaspoons ground fennel

3 teaspoons chopped
   thyme or ¼ teaspoon
   dried thyme (see Note)

2 teaspoons apple
   cider vinegar

½ teaspoon sea salt

These delicious savoury rolls are filled with the flavour of fresh fennel, onion, apple and herbs and the cottage cheese gives a sublime creamy texture. They make a substantial meal served with a really good tomato chutney or sauce.

~~~~~~~~

To make the filling

Heat the oil in a heavy-based saucepan over medium–low heat and sauté the onion, fennel and garlic until softened. Remove from the pan and set aside to cool.

Place the bacon in the same pan and sauté until lightly browned. Remove from the pan and set aside to cool.

In a large bowl, use a large metal spoon or your hands to mix together the remaining filling ingredients with the cooled fennel, onion, garlic and bacon, making sure that the mixture is very well combined.

Preheat the oven to 200°C (400°F). Line two baking trays with baking paper.

To assemble for baking

Cut each pastry sheet in half lengthways and brush down one long edge of each piece with some of the egg wash.

Divide the filling into four equal amounts. Use your hands to form each portion into a sausage shape long enough to fit the pieces of pastry, then place along the longer dry edge of each.

Roll up the pastry from the dry edge to the wet and seal, then position the rolls on the trays so that they are seam side down. Cut each long roll into 3 pieces. Prick each piece twice with a fork or the point of a sharp knife.

Brush with the egg wash and sprinkle with the poppy seeds (if using).

Bake for 15–20 minutes, or until puffed and golden brown.

NOTE *Lemon thyme is especially delicious in this recipe.*

Cheesy Meatballs with Tomato Chilli Glaze

SERVES 4

50 ml (1½ fl oz) extra virgin olive oil

3 packaged tasty cheese slices

FOR THE MEATBALLS

300 g (10½ oz) beef sausage mince

300 g (10½ oz) beef mince

60 g (2¼ oz) soft ricotta

150 g (5½ oz) onion, coarsely grated

1 garlic clove, crushed

2 teaspoons chutney

2 teaspoons soy sauce

3 teaspoons barbecue sauce

3 teaspoons tomato sauce (ketchup)

50 g (1¾ oz) fresh breadcrumbs

½ teaspoon sea salt

FOR THE GLAZE

3 teaspoons tomato paste (concentrated purée)

60 ml (2 fl oz) dry white wine or Apera

2 teaspoons soy sauce

30 ml (1 fl oz) sweet chilli sauce

30 ml (1 fl oz) barbecue sauce

These meatballs are a crowd-pleaser for people of any age. They are topped with cheese and basted with a mild tomato chilli sauce, which forms a lovely tasty glaze. They can be served as a canapé, used to fill crusty bread rolls or served with vegetables or salad for a main meal.

Preheat the oven to 180°C (350°F). Pour the oil into a 20 x 30 cm (8 x 12 inch) baking dish.

To make the meatballs

Place the meatball ingredients in a large bowl and mix until very well combined. Shape into 18–20 walnut-sized balls.

To make the glaze

Mix the glaze ingredients in a small bowl with 150 ml (5 fl oz) water and stir until well combined. Set aside.

To bake

Heat the dish in the oven for 5 minutes, then remove. Place the meatballs in the hot dish and use tongs to carefully coat them in the oil. Return the dish to the oven and bake for 10 minutes.

Reduce the oven temperature to 170°C (325°F).

Meanwhile, cut the cheese slices into enough pieces to top each meatball with a portion.

Remove the dish from the oven and top each meatball with a piece of cheese.

Bake for 5 minutes, then remove the dish from the oven. Use a spoon to remove the excess fat from the pan and discard, then carefully pour the glaze over the meatballs.

Bake for 10 minutes, or until the meatballs are cooked through and the sauce has reduced a little.

Stuffed Mushroom Bread Cups with Chorizo Crumb

MAKES 12

125 g (4½ oz) basil pesto

6 cherry tomatoes

FOR THE BREAD CUPS

12 slices white or wholemeal bread (sandwich slice thickness), crusts removed

olive oil cooking spray

FOR THE FILLING

2 teaspoons extra virgin olive oil

100 g (3½ oz) chorizo, skin removed and finely chopped

250 g (9 oz) large button mushrooms, with 5 cm (2 inch) cups

80 g (2¾ oz) fresh breadcrumbs

1 egg, lightly whisked

10 sage leaves, finely chopped

3 teaspoons dry white wine or Apera

1 teaspoon worcestershire sauce

2 teaspoons lemon juice

pinch of sea salt (optional)

NOTE *I recently found crumbed chorizo at my local store – it's such a time-saving product if you can get it. If using a regular chorizo, remove the skin and finely chop the sausage.*

From the crunch of the bread cases to the bright pop of pesto, these rich and crispy morsels topped with chorizo are sure to be a dinner party favourite. The bold sharpness of basil combined with the earthy, minty tones of sage are a wonderful marriage of flavours. I happened upon the combination when walking past my sage bush during the development of this recipe; plucking and tearing a leaf and realising that its aroma was intoxicating and most pleasing. It could well be my new favourite herb.

~~~~~~

To make the bread cups

Preheat the oven to 170°C (325°F).

Use a rolling pin to roll each slice of bread out thinly. Cut an 8 cm (3¼ inch) circle from each slice to fit the holes of a 12 x 50 ml (1½ fl oz) muffin or tart tin.

Spray the bread circles sparingly with the olive oil on both sides and press into the tins.

Bake for 10 minutes, or until golden and crisp. Remove the bread cups from the tins and leave to cool on a wire rack.

To make the filling

Heat the oil in a heavy-based frying pan. Sauté the chorizo until it's starting to crisp. Remove the pan from the heat.

Wipe the mushrooms and remove the stalks. Cut a tiny sliver from the bottom of each stalk and discard, then chop the stalks finely.

Remove half of the chorizo from the pan and set aside.

To the chorizo remaining in the pan, add the chopped mushroom stalks, breadcrumbs, egg, sage, wine, worcestershire sauce and lemon juice and a little salt if desired.

To assemble for baking

Preheat the oven to 170°C (325°F).

Place the bread cups back in the muffin tin holes and spoon a teaspoon of pesto into the base of each. Fill the mushroom caps with the filling mixture, mounding up as required. Place a filled mushroom on top of the pesto, then gently press the reserved chorizo on top. Cut the cherry tomatoes in half and place one, cut side down, on top of each of the filled mushrooms.

Bake for 15–20 minutes, or until crisp and golden and the tomatoes begin to blister. Leave to stand in the tins for 3 minutes, then carefully transfer to a wire rack. Serve immediately.

Wildlife on the Patch

When we first moved to the Derwent Valley the marauding wildlife came as quite a shock. At our former home by the ocean at Eaglehawk Neck, only a few possums caused an issue. I was told by the locals that if you feed one, then it would become protective and keep others away. I used to bake Anzac biscuits for a beautiful possum that visited our balcony each night and the plan really seemed to work.

That was not the case here, however – the possum population seemed to be much larger, and that's not to mention the number of hungry wallabies and potoroos. Raspberry canes, vegetables and even rhubarb crowns were eaten into the ground. I would never shoot the poor creatures, nor relocate them, which is apparently a cruel practice and besides, it just means that others of their relatives move in.

I listened avidly to all advice on gardening programs and read innumerable articles on the topic. A floppy chicken wire fence was the first recommendation. The possums soon worked out how to overcome that obstacle.

An electric fence was the second attempt – we were then told (after significant financial outlay and effort) that this doesn't work with possums as their fur is so thick that the current doesn't penetrate. This seemed to be the case as they weren't deterred at all.

Then there was the suggestion to get bags of dog clippings from a pet groomer. When I asked at one establishment, they looked at me as if I was rather peculiar – I quickly left and didn't try that tactic again.

LED flashing Christmas lights? The expectation was high, so we bought several hundred metres of them to top the orchard fence. We were assured that would definitely work. It didn't. When we told a friend we'd installed them, they simply said: 'That just tells the possums where the party is!' And so it was.

Nowadays we have come to accept that we have to live with them. After all, we are the interlopers. They can't read the human rule book – they must think we provide a lovely smorgasbord for them. And we know that all edible plants must be covered, even aromatic herbs.

I have had one small victory of sorts, though. I planted Tasmanian native pepperberry bushes, which now thrive along the side of the cooking school – possums, wallabies and potoroos don't touch them.

The bushes produce far too many berries for us to eat – though I do dry and grind some to sprinkle over breads and other bakes. However, they provide winter fodder for currawongs who come along in twos or threes, with one of them standing guard on the wires above. After a week or so they have had their fill and then dozens of tiny birds come in to eat the remainder. I consider it to be a pretty fair compromise, all things considered.

Spinach, Goat's Cheese & Roasted Tomato Tarts

MAKES 12

FOR THE PASTRY

120 g (4¼ oz) plain (all-purpose) flour

20 g (¾ oz) self-raising flour

½ teaspoon sea salt

70 g (2½ oz) cold salted butter, diced

45 g (1½ oz) natural or Greek-style yoghurt

FOR THE FILLING

200 g (7 oz) cherry tomatoes

2 teaspoons extra virgin olive oil

120 g (4¼ oz) spinach or silverbeet (Swiss chard) leaves, washed and finely sliced

90 ml (3 fl oz) milk

2 teaspoons cornflour (cornstarch)

5 eggs, lightly whisked

¼ teaspoon sea salt (optional)

2 spring onions (scallions), finely sliced

1 garlic clove, crushed

110 g (3¾ oz) goat's cheese, crumbled

60 g (2¼ oz) parmesan, finely grated

In these tarts the sharpness of the goat's cheese is counterbalanced with the sweetness of baked and blistered cherry tomatoes. Served hot, warm or cold, these tasty tarts are a delightful snack.

To make the pastry

Place the flours, salt and butter in a food processor and process until the mixture resembles breadcrumbs. (Alternatively, this can be achieved by rubbing the ingredients together with your fingers.) Transfer to a large bowl and make a well in the centre.

In a separate bowl, whisk together the yoghurt with 40 ml (1¼ fl oz) cold water.

Add enough of the yogurt mixture to the flour to make a soft dough, adding extra liquid if needed. Wrap in plastic wrap and place in the fridge for at least 30 minutes to firm up before using.

To make the filling

Preheat the oven to 200°C (400°F). Place the tomatoes in an ovenproof dish and drizzle with the olive oil. Bake for 10 minutes, or until the tomatoes have softened a little and the skin blisters. Set aside to cool, leaving the oven on.

Place the spinach or silverbeet in a heatproof bowl. Pour boiling water over the leaves, then leave to stand for 1 minute before draining in a colander and leaving to cool. Place on paper towel and squeeze out any excess liquid (see Note).

In a small bowl, whisk together the milk with the cornflour to make a paste, then whisk in the eggs and salt (if using). Stir in the spring onion and garlic. Transfer to a jug and set aside.

To assemble for baking

Grease 12 x 50 ml (1½ fl oz) tart tins or a 12-hole muffin tin.

Roll the pastry out thinly on a lightly floured surface. Cut circles to fit the base and side of the tins and press into place.

Distribute the goat's cheese, tomatoes and blanched leaves evenly between the pastry cases and then carefully pour the egg mixture over the top. Sprinkle with the parmesan.

Bake for 5 minutes, then reduce the oven temperature to 150°C (300°F) and bake for 10 minutes more, or until the filling has set. Leave to stand in the tins for 5–10 minutes, then carefully transfer to a wire rack.

NOTE *Reserve the liquid drained from the spinach or silverbeet and refrigerate to use later in soups and gravies.*

Baby Yorkshire Puddings with Smoked Salmon & Chives

MAKES 12

FOR THE PUDDINGS

120 g (4¼ oz) plain (all-purpose) flour

40 g (1½ oz) self-raising flour

2 eggs

125 ml (4 fl oz) milk

½ teaspoon sea salt

FOR THE FILLING

200 g (7 oz) cream cheese, softened

50 g (1¾ oz) sour cream

3 teaspoons lemon juice

2 teaspoons mayonnaise

1 teaspoon dijon mustard

2 tablespoons snipped chives

3 teaspoons chopped dill, plus 2 teaspoons extra for garnish (optional)

40 g (1½ oz) capers, roughly chopped, plus 20 g (¾ oz) capers extra

200 g (7 oz) smoked salmon, diced, plus 50 g (1¾ oz) extra sliced into strips

Yorkshire puddings would arguably be one of the most popular of baked goods. In this recipe the centre of the golden, crisp crust contains a sumptuous creamy smoked salmon filling flavoured with capers, chives and lemon.

The puddings can be served as a canapé, an entree or even a substantial snack.

To make the puddings

Place the pudding ingredients in a bowl with 125 ml (4 fl oz) cold water and whisk until smooth. Leave to stand for 1 hour (this is not absolutely necessary but gives a better result).

When ready to bake, preheat the oven to 210°C (410°F). Brush vegetable oil in a 12-hole x 50 ml (1½ fl oz) muffin tin. Place the tin in the oven to heat for 5 minutes.

Stir the pudding mixture once more and then carefully ladle it into the hot tin.

Bake for 20–25 minutes, or until nicely browned and puffed. Do not open the oven door during this time.

Remove from the oven and leave to stand in the tin for 2 minutes before transferring to a wire rack to cool.

To make the filling

Whisk together the cream cheese, sour cream, lemon juice, mayonnaise and mustard. Stir in the chives, dill (if using), the 40 g of chopped capers and the 200 g (7 oz) of diced smoked salmon. Season to taste with salt and freshly ground black pepper.

To assemble

By now the puddings will likely have collapsed a little (if not, scoop out a small spoonful from the centre).

Spoon the filling into the cases.

Garnish the top of each pudding with the remaining capers, smoked salmon strips and dill (if using).

Chicken, Halloumi & Roasted Capsicum Parcels

SERVES 6

12 ready-rolled filo pastry sheets (from the refrigerated section of the supermarket)

125 ml (4 fl oz) extra virgin olive oil

1 egg, lightly whisked

50 g (1¾ oz) sesame seeds

FOR THE FILLING

2 teaspoons paprika

2 teaspoons ground cumin

1 teaspoon ground coriander

¼ teaspoon ground cardamom, plus a large pinch extra

¼ teaspoon sumac, plus a large pinch extra

½ teaspoon sea salt

½ teaspoon white (granulated) sugar

500 g (1 lb 2 oz) skinless chicken breasts

30 ml (1 fl oz) extra virgin olive oil

160 g (5¾ oz) halloumi, cut into 6 mm (¼ inch) wide strips

250 g (9 oz) roasted red capsicum (pepper) halves

200 g (7 oz) natural or Greek-style yoghurt

50 g (1¾ oz) cream cheese, softened

1 garlic clove, crushed

3 teaspoons cornflour (cornstarch)

2 teaspoons sweet chilli sauce

2 teaspoons lemon juice

pinch of sea salt

The flavours of the Middle East feature in these mouth-watering parcels. For this recipe I buy bottled roasted red capsicums (peppers). While you could prepare your own, it is a time-consuming step.

To make the filling

Prepare a spice mix by combining the paprika, cumin, coriander, cardamom, sumac, salt and sugar.

Cut the chicken breasts into 5 cm (2 inch) strips and place in a bowl. Sprinkle with the spice mixture and then mix well to coat evenly.

Heat the oil in a frying pan over medium heat and sauté the chicken for 2 minutes each side. Remove to a plate.

Place the halloumi in the same pan and fry for 1–2 minutes on both sides, or until golden brown. Remove from the heat.

Pat the capsicum halves dry with paper towel and cut into 4 cm (1½ inch) strips.

In a bowl, whisk the yoghurt, cream cheese, garlic, cornflour, chilli sauce, lemon juice, extra cardamom, extra sumac and salt until the mixture is smooth.

To assemble for baking

Preheat the oven to 200°C (400°F). Line a large baking tray with baking paper.

Place one sheet of filo on a lightly floured surface, then brush with some of the olive oil. Fold in half. Brush another sheet with oil, then fold in half and place on top of the first folded sheet.

Spoon a scant ¼ cup of the yoghurt mixture onto the filo, leaving an 8 mm (⅜ inch) edge dry.

Top with one sixth of the chicken strips, halloumi and, finally, the capsicum strips.

Brush the dry edge with the whisked egg to seal, then carefully roll up to enclose the filling. Place on the tray seam side down.

Repeat to make six parcels in total.

Mix 2 teaspoons water into the remaining whisked egg and brush over each parcel to glaze. Sprinkle with the sesame seeds.

Bake for 20 minutes, or until the parcels are golden brown and crisp.

Beef & Beer Pies with Pea Purée

MAKES 8

1 egg yolk whisked with 20 ml (½ fl oz) water, for glaze

2 sheets ready-rolled puff pastry, thawed

FOR THE PASTRY

250 g (9 oz) plain (all-purpose) flour

¼ teaspoon baking powder

½ teaspoon sea salt

125 g (4½ oz) cold salted butter, diced

1 egg yolk lightly whisked with 80 ml (2½ fl oz) cold milk

FOR THE FILLING

20 ml (½ fl oz) extra virgin olive oil

800 g (1 lb 12 oz) beef mince

100 g (3½ oz) rindless bacon, diced

1 onion, finely diced

½ teaspoon curry powder

30 g (1 oz) tomato sauce (ketchup)

3 teaspoons worcestershire sauce

2 teaspoons soy sauce

20 g (¾ oz) tomato relish

½ teaspoon sea salt

375 ml (13 fl oz) beer

3–4 teaspoons cornflour (cornstarch) mixed to a paste with 40 ml (1¼ fl oz) cold water

FOR THE PEA PURÉE

400 g (14 oz) fresh or frozen peas

2 spring onions (scallions), white part only, roughly chopped

3 teaspoons lemon juice

125 ml (4 fl oz) pouring cream

1 egg white, lightly whisked

These pies encapsulate the Australian tradition of the pie floater – beer, pies and tasty pea purée – but they are far more transportable.

To make the pastry

Place the dry ingredients and butter in a food processor and process until the mixture resembles breadcrumbs. (Alternatively, this can be achieved by rubbing the ingredients together with your fingers.) Transfer to a large bowl and mix with enough of the egg mixture to make a soft dough. Wrap in plastic wrap and place in the fridge for at least 30 minutes to firm up before using.

To make the filling

Heat the oil in a heavy-based saucepan over medium–high heat and cook the beef with the bacon until well coloured, around 10 minutes. Add the onion and curry powder and cook for 3 minutes more. Add the sauces and relish, salt and beer. Bring to the boil, then reduce the heat and gently simmer uncovered for 20 minutes. Gradually stir in enough of the cornflour paste to reach a thick consistency. Set aside to cool.

To make the pea purée

Cook the peas in boiling salted water for 3–5 minutes until just tender. Drain, then immediately plunge into cold water so that they hold their colour. Drain again. Cool slightly, then, using a stick blender, purée with the spring onion, lemon juice, cream and egg white.

To assemble

Preheat the oven to 200°C (400°F). Grease eight 200 ml (7 fl oz) pie tins.

Remove the pastry from the fridge and roll out to 3 mm (⅛ inch) on a lightly floured surface. Cut out eight 12 cm (4½ inch) circles to fit the base and side of the tins and press into place. Brush the pastry edges generously with some of the whisked egg glaze. Divide the meat mixture between the tins and spread out evenly. Top with the pea purée.

Cut eight circles from the puff pastry sheets to fit amply over the top of the pies. Crimp the edges with your fingers or a fork to seal. Whisk 3 teaspoons water into the remaining egg glaze and brush on the tops of the pies. Prick each pie twice with the tip of a sharp knife.

Bake for 20–25 minutes, or until the pastry is golden brown. Leave to stand in the tins for 5 minutes, then carefully transfer to a wire rack.

NOTE The filling and pea purée can be made up to 2 days in advance. Refrigerate as soon as they are cool.

Egg & Bacon Tarts

MAKES 12

3 sheets ready-rolled
   puff pastry, thawed

250 g (9 oz) rindless bacon,
   diced

12 eggs

90 g (3¼ oz) tasty cheese,
   grated

The saltiness of bacon, the creaminess of cheese . . . these make for delicious small morsels, ideal for a snack or a lunch box addition.

   The eggs are not slashed or mixed together as with some versions of this recipe – rather the yolks are left whole. I've found it gives a much better result in that the all-too-often rubbery texture is avoided and, if you time it really well, the yolk may well retain a measure of softness, which is most pleasing. Best of all, these tarts are simple to make.

~~~~~~~~

Preheat the oven to 200°C (400°F). Grease a 12-hole x 80 ml (2½ fl oz) muffin tin.

Cut four 12 cm (4½ inch) circles from each pastry sheet to fit the base and side of the muffin holes and press into place.

Sprinkle half the bacon evenly over the bases. Break an egg into each pastry case. Sprinkle the remaining bacon evenly over the eggs. Sprinkle on the cheese.

Bake for 12–15 minutes, or until the pastry is golden brown and the eggs are just set.

Leave to stand in the tin for 5 minutes before removing to a wire rack, or serve immediately.

Mexican Meat Turnovers

MAKES 20

5 sheets ready-rolled puff pastry, thawed

1 egg yolk whisked with 20 ml (½ fl oz) water, for glaze

80 g (2¾ oz) tasty cheddar cheese, feta or mozzarella, cut into 20 small cubes (see Note)

FOR THE FILLING

20 ml (½ fl oz) extra virgin olive oil

400 g (14 oz) beef mince

250 g (9 oz) onion, finely diced

3 garlic cloves, crushed

3 teaspoons ground cumin

3 teaspoons ground coriander

½–1 teaspoon chilli flakes

½ teaspoon smoked paprika

1 teaspoon dried oregano

60 g (2¼ oz) tomato paste (concentrated purée)

40 ml (1¼ fl oz) dry red wine

20 ml (½ fl oz) sweet chilli sauce

20 g (¾ oz) semi-dried tomatoes, finely chopped (optional)

2 teaspoons red wine vinegar (or apple cider vinegar)

400 g (14 oz) tin diced tomatoes or diced fresh tomatoes

½ teaspoon sea salt

¼ teaspoon soft brown sugar

½ teaspoon white (granulated) sugar

3 teaspoons cornflour (cornstarch) mixed to a paste with 40 ml (1¼ fl oz) cold water

The beef in these empanadas is subtly spiced, however, more chilli can be added to suit your personal preference. The small amount of cheese in each empanada is a creamy counterbalance to the robust flavour of the meat and the crispiness of the pastry.

While ready-rolled puff pastry sheets are used here, a homemade Easy Flaky Pastry could be prepared instead (see recipe on page 226).

To make the filling

Heat the oil in a heavy-based saucepan over medium–high heat and sauté the beef until well coloured, 5–10 minutes.

Add the onion and cook for 5 minutes more. Add the garlic, spices, oregano and tomato paste and cook for 1 minute more.

Stir in the red wine, chilli sauce, semi-dried tomatoes (if using), vinegar, tomatoes, salt and sugars. Bring to the boil, then reduce the heat and simmer uncovered for 20 minutes.

Gradually stir in enough cornflour paste to reach a thick consistency. Set aside to cool.

To assemble

Preheat the oven to 200°C (400°F). Line two baking trays with baking paper.

Cut four 10 cm (4 inch) circles from each pastry sheet, then brush the pastry with some of the egg wash.

Spoon 1 tablespoon of the filling into the centre of each circle. Place a cube of cheese on top.

Fold the circles in half to enclose the filling. Crimp the edges together with your fingers or a fork to firmly seal. Brush with the egg wash.

Place on the trays and bake for 15–20 minutes, or until golden brown.

NOTE *Mexican varieties of cheese could be used in this recipe, if available, but a tasty cheddar, feta or mozzarella are good, and perhaps more accessible, substitutes.*

Individual Seafood Pies

MAKES 8

1 egg, lightly whisked,
  for glaze

FOR THE PASTRY

350 g (12 oz) plain
  (all-purpose) flour

½ teaspoon baking powder

½ teaspoon sea salt

180 g (6½ oz) cold salted
  butter, diced

FOR THE FILLING

45 g (1½ oz) salted butter

200 g (7 oz) boneless,
  skinless salmon fillets

80 g (2¾ oz) boneless,
  skinless white fish
  fillet, such as ling

40 ml (1¼ fl oz) dry white wine

450 ml (16 fl oz) milk

3 teaspoons cornflour
  (cornstarch) mixed to
  a paste with 50 ml
  (1½ fl oz) milk

2 teaspoons lemon or lime juice

2 teaspoons mayonnaise

1 spring onion (scallion),
  finely chopped,
  white part only

1 teaspoon chopped dill
  (optional)

½ teaspoon sea salt

250 g (9 oz) scallops, cleaned

100 g (3½ oz) small cooked
  prawns, peeled and deveined

NOTE *If time is short, ready-rolled sheets of shortcrust pastry can be substituted for this homemade version.*

These pies combine seafood with a creamy sauce inside a buttery shortcrust pastry. I like to use salmon for its colour, a little white fish (such as ling) for its texture, and scallops and prawns for sheer luxury.

~~~~~~~~

To make the pastry

Place the dry ingredients and butter in a food processor and process until the mixture resembles breadcrumbs. (Alternatively, this can be achieved by rubbing the ingredients together with your fingers.) Transfer to a bowl and mix in enough cold water – around 120 ml (4 fl oz) – to make a soft dough. Wrap in plastic wrap and place in the fridge for at least 30 minutes to firm up before using.

To make the filling

Melt the butter in a frying pan and gently sauté the salmon and white fish over medium–low heat for 4 minutes on one side, then 2 minutes on the other. Set the fish aside on a plate. Once cooled, break into bite-sized pieces.

Pour the wine into the same pan that you cooked the salmon in and stir over medium–low heat to deglaze. Remove from the heat and add the milk and cornflour paste. Put the pan back over the heat and bring to a simmer, whisking until the sauce reaches a thick custard consistency. Remove from the heat and stir in the lemon or lime juice, mayonnaise, spring onion, dill (if using) and salt. Place a piece of baking paper on the surface to stop a skin forming. Set aside to cool.

In a separate heatproof bowl, pour boiling water over the scallops and prawns. Stand for 30 seconds, then drain well.

When the sauce has cooled, add the salmon, white fish and seafood.

To assemble for baking

Preheat the oven to 200°C (400°F). Grease eight 200–250 ml (7–9 oz) pie tins, preferably with a removable base. On a lightly floured surface, roll the pastry out to 3 mm (⅛ inch) thick. Cut eight circles to fit the base and side of the tins and press into place. Brush the surface with the whisked egg to seal (you'll have some egg wash left over). Re-roll the pastry if needed and cut eight slightly smaller circles to fit the tops. Divide the filling evenly between the bases, place the pastry lids on top and crimp the edges together with your fingers or a fork to firmly seal.

Add 3 teaspoons cold water to the remaining whisked egg and brush over the pies to glaze. (If extra is needed whisk 1 egg yolk with 3 teaspoons water.) Prick each pie twice with the tip of a sharp knife.

Bake the pies for 20 minutes, or until the pastry is golden. Leave to stand in the tins for 5 minutes, then carefully transfer to a wire rack.

Large
Savouries

Creamy Potato Bake

SERVES 6–8

3 garlic cloves, crushed

¾ teaspoon sea salt

600 ml (21 fl oz) pouring cream

1 teaspoon dijon mustard

3 teaspoons mayonnaise

2 teaspoons cornflour
(cornstarch)

950 g (2 lb 2 oz) peeled
potatoes (see Note)

400 g (14 oz) onions or
4–6 spring onions (scallions),
finely diced

3 teaspoons chopped
rosemary or oregano

200 g (7 oz) rindless bacon,
diced

100 g (3½ oz) tasty cheese,
grated

This dish is full of oozy, creamy luxury with the flavours of onion, chives, bacon and mustard. It's a special occasion dish that encapsulates the spirit of comfort baking.

Preheat the oven to 170°C (325°F). Grease a 25 x 35 cm (10 x 14 inch) baking dish, 8 cm (3¼ inches) deep.

In a bowl or jug, whisk the garlic, salt, cream, mustard, mayonnaise and cornflour until smooth.

Cut the potatoes into 6 mm (¼ inch) slices.

Drizzle 50 ml (1½ fl oz) of the cream mixture into the base of the dish. Layer one-third of the potato over this, then top with half the onion, sprinkle with half the herbs and then one-quarter of the bacon. Pour 180 ml (6 fl oz) of the cream mixture on top.

Repeat the layers. Top with the last of the potato and drizzle on the remaining cream mixture. Sprinkle on the last of the bacon and top with the cheese.

Bake for 1 hour, or until the potato is cooked.

Leave to stand for 10 minutes before serving.

NOTE *The potatoes do not necessarily have to be peeled.*

Spinach & Ricotta Tart

SERVES 6–8

2 sheets ready-rolled
  puff pastry, thawed

FOR THE FILLING

600 g (1 lb 5 oz) shredded spinach
  or silverbeet (Swiss chard) leaves
  (weight after stalks removed)

500 g (1 lb 2 oz) soft ricotta

125 g (4½ oz) sliced bread
  (weight with crusts removed),
  cut into 4 cm (1½ inch) squares

125 ml (4 fl oz) milk

14 eggs

90 g (3¼ oz) parmesan,
  finely grated

200 g (7 oz) Greek-style feta,
  crumbled

1 tablespoon chopped
  flat-leaf parsley (optional)

3 teaspoons chopped
  oregano or ¼ teaspoon
  dried oregano

1 tablespoon finely
  snipped chives

60 g (2¼ oz) tasty cheese,
  grated, plus 80 g
  (2¾ oz) extra

This tart is a step above the regular spinach and ricotta tart in that eggs with unbroken yolks are nestled among the tasty filling. Optimum visual results are achieved by using the best quality free-range eggs. Delicious served hot or cold, it's definitely a dish to share with friends.

Preheat the oven to 200°C (400°F). Grease a 23 x 10 cm (9 x 4 inch) round springform cake tin.

Line the tin with the pastry sheets, joining in the middle and then trimming off the excess at the rim. Brush the edges with a little water.

Place the spinach or silverbeet in a heatproof bowl. Pour boiling water over the leaves, then leave to stand for 2 minutes before draining in a colander and leaving to cool. Place on paper towel and squeeze out any excess liquid.

Meanwhile, place the ricotta on two sheets of paper towel and leave to stand in a colander for 5 minutes to remove excess liquid.

Place the bread slices in a bowl and pour the milk over the top. Leave to stand for 5 minutes, then squeeze out the excess liquid.

In a large bowl, whisk together six of the eggs, then add the cooled spinach or silverbeet, drained ricotta, soaked bread, parmesan, feta, herbs and the 60 g (2¼ oz) of tasty cheese.

Spoon the filling into the pastry crust. Make small indents (as far as it's possible) and break the remaining eight eggs into these.

Sprinkle on the remaining grated tasty cheese and bake for 10 minutes, then reduce the oven temperature to 160°C (315°F) and bake for 50 minutes, or until the filling is set.

Leave to stand for at least 15 minutes before cutting into slices to serve.

Classic Quiche

SERVES 6

120 g (4¼ oz) tasty
cheese, grated

60 g (2¼ oz) parmesan,
finely grated

FOR THE PASTRY

180 g (6½ oz) plain
(all-purpose) flour

¼ teaspoon sea salt

¼ teaspoon baking powder

90 g (3¼ oz) cold salted
butter, diced

FOR THE FILLING

190 ml (6½ fl oz) pouring
cream (you can substitute
the cream with 190 ml extra
milk or 180 g/6½ oz creamed
corn if you wish)

190 ml (6½ fl oz) milk

6 eggs

2 teaspoons mayonnaise

1 teaspoon dijon mustard

pinch of sea salt

**When people come to call, it's always good to have something in
your cooking repertoire that is tasty and can easily be prepared.
This recipe can be made from some simple basic ingredients or lifted
to a higher level by using more luxurious items such as smoked
salmon or pancetta. While the recipe for a quick pastry is given here,
it is perfectly acceptable to use ready-rolled commercially prepared
puff or shortcrust pastry instead.**

To make the pastry

Place the dry ingredients and butter in a food processor and process
until the mixture resembles fine breadcrumbs. (Alternatively, this can
be achieved by rubbing the ingredients together with your fingers.)

Transfer to a bowl and make a well in the centre. Drizzle in enough
cold water – around 80 ml (2½ fl oz) – to just bring it together to make
a soft dough. Don't add more water than is necessary or it will become
too wet.

Turn out onto a lightly floured surface and flatten out to a rectangle
1 cm (½ inch) thick. Wrap in plastic wrap and place in the fridge for
at least 30 minutes to firm up before using.

To make the filling

Whisk the filling ingredients together until well combined, then
set aside.

To assemble for baking

Preheat the oven to 200°C (400°F). Grease a 23 cm (9 inch) round tart
plate or tin, 6 cm (2½ inches) deep.

On a lightly floured surface, roll the pastry out to cover the base and
side of the tart plate and press into place. (If using a ready-rolled puff
or shortcrust pastry sheet, roll it out until it is large enough for the
tart plate.)

Sprinkle 50 g (1¾ oz) of the tasty cheese over the base and top with
your selected additional fillings, if using (see opposite). Top this with
almost all the remaining tasty cheese and the parmesan. Pour the wet
filling mixture carefully on top. Lastly, top with the remaining cheese.

Bake for 10 minutes, then reduce the oven temperature to 160°C
(315°F) and bake for 30 minutes more, or until the filling is just set.

Leave to stand for 10 minutes before cutting.

Additional optional fillings

A quiche is such a versatile dish: the filling combinations are almost endless. Choose up to two of these additional fillings to add to the base with the tasty cheese.

90 g (3¼ oz) roasted cherry tomatoes

90 g (3¼ oz) roasted cubed pumpkin (squash)

herbs such as basil, flat-leaf parsley or thyme, to taste

125 g (4½ oz) sautéed leek or onion

2 spring onions (scallions), chopped

125 g (4½ oz) corn kernels

150 g (5½ oz) asparagus, tinned or poached fresh

125 g (4½ oz) smoked salmon, cut into small pieces

125 g (4½ oz) diced ham, rindless bacon or pancetta

150 g (5½ oz) shredded spinach or silverbeet
(Swiss chard) leaves, blanched (see page 140)

NOTE *Any left-over pastry can be refrigerated for 2 days or frozen for up to 3 months.*

Eggs

It is often stated that the best of ingredients give the best results. While I agree with this to a point, I have spent many years experimenting with the least expensive of basic ingredients such as flour, sugar and butter, to actually measure the level of difference. Really, it has to be said, that it is negligible, if any.

However, one ingredient I am particular about is eggs. Just compare a custard or cake batter made with truly free-range eggs to those made with eggs from caged birds, and the difference is clearly evident.

It's not only the colour; the egg will also perform much better – cakes will rise well, have greater stability, improved texture and flavour.

I've noticed this especially since keeping our own chickens here on the farm.

They are a cunning group of girls. Well aware that we collect their eggs each day, they have developed a tactic to outsmart us when they think it's time to hatch some chicks.

They lay a clutch of eggs over the fence, camouflaged in the scrub of the neighbour's property. Enough of the other hens keep producing their eggs in the usual places that we are unaware of this strategy until it's too late.

The mother hens bring their hatched brood back while they are still small enough to fit through the holes in the chicken-wire fence. Before you know it, they have arrived to stay, usually a dozen or more chicks at a time. It's a conspiracy.

From then on it's a battle for the mothers to keep their babies from the marauding currawongs and eagles, but they usually succeed and our flock of hens keeps growing exponentially.

Sometimes the quantity of the eggs is an issue – there are dozens and dozens of them, more than I can ever use even with my excessive baking habits. We share them around to friends, family and anyone who comes to visit.

Without exception, all who receive them later comment about the quality of any dish that has been made with them – from simple scrambled eggs through to cakes, bakes and custards.

So my advice is – bake with the best eggs you can possibly get. You will be rewarded with a far better result than those from hens kept in poor conditions.

Salmon, Sweetcorn & Asparagus Quiche

SERVES 6–8

FOR THE PASTRY

200 g (7 oz) plain (all-purpose) flour

¼ teaspoon baking powder

¼ teaspoon sea salt

100 g (3½ oz) cold salted butter

1 spring onion (scallion), chopped

1 egg yolk, lightly whisked

70 ml (2¼ fl oz) milk

FOR THE FILLING

30 g (1 oz) salted butter

400 g (14 oz) boneless, skinless salmon fillets

60 ml (2 fl oz) dry white wine

4 eggs

400 g (14 oz) creamed corn

3 teaspoons mayonnaise

20 ml (½ fl oz) lemon juice

2 teaspoons cornflour (cornstarch)

125 g (4½ oz) sour cream

¼–½ teaspoon sea salt (optional)

300 g (10½ oz) tinned asparagus spears or steamed asparagus, well drained and cut into 1.5 cm (⅝ inch) lengths

1 spring onion (scallion), finely chopped

150 g (5½ oz) tasty cheese, grated, plus 10 g (¼ oz) extra

60 g (2¼ oz) parmesan, finely grated

Delicious and generous chunks of butter-poached salmon are complemented by the earthiness of asparagus and corn in this delicious quiche.

To make the pastry

Place the flour, baking powder, salt, butter and spring onion in a food processor and process until the mixture resembles breadcrumbs. (Alternatively, this can be achieved by rubbing the ingredients together with your fingers.)

Whisk together the egg yolk and milk until just combined.

Transfer the flour mixture to a large bowl, make a well in the centre and pour in almost all of the egg mixture. Mix with a metal spoon to form a soft dough, adding the remaining liquid if necessary. (Extra milk may even be needed.) Wrap in plastic wrap and place in the fridge for at least 30 minutes to firm up before using.

To make the filling

Melt the butter in a frying pan over medium–low heat and cook the salmon for 2 minutes on each side. Remove from the pan and set aside.

Pour the white wine into the pan and stir to deglaze over medium heat for 1 minute, then remove from the heat.

In a bowl or jug, whisk together the eggs, creamed corn, mayonnaise, lemon juice, cornflour, sour cream and salt (if using). Strain the white wine mixture into this and stir to combine.

To assemble for baking

Preheat the oven to 200°C (400°F). Grease a 23 cm (9 inch) round tart plate or tin, 8 cm (3¼ inches) deep.

On a lightly floured surface, roll out the pastry to fit the base and side of the tart plate and press into place, leaving a little overhang for the time being.

Break the salmon into 1 cm (½ inch) chunks and distribute evenly over the pastry case. Place the asparagus and spring onion evenly around the salmon. Sprinkle with the tasty cheese and the parmesan. Gently pour the filling on top and finish by sprinkling with the extra tasty cheese. Trim the overhanging pastry.

Bake for 10 minutes, then reduce the oven temperature to 140°C (275°F) and bake for 40 minutes more, or until the filling is set. Remove from the oven and leave to stand for 15 minutes before cutting into slices to serve.

Sweet Potato Slice

SERVES 6–8

90 g (3¼ oz) silverbeet
  (Swiss chard), kale
  or spinach leaves

6 eggs

400 g (14 oz) peeled sweet potato,
  cut into 1 cm (½ inch) cubes

1 onion, roughly chopped

1½ tablespoons finely chopped
  flat-leaf parsley

1 teaspoon chopped
  oregano leaves

250 g (9 oz) ham or rindless
  bacon, diced

250 g (9 oz) tasty cheese, grated

150 g (5½ oz) self-raising flour

125 ml (4 fl oz) extra virgin
  olive oil

½ –1 teaspoon sea salt

In this nourishing and flavoursome dish, sweet potato matches perfectly with the saltiness of ham or bacon and cheese and the zest of fresh herbs. It is delicious served hot but equally so when cold; it is therefore a perfect addition to a lunch box the next day.

~~~~~~~~~

Preheat the oven to 170°C (325°F). Grease a 20 x 35 cm (8 x 14 inch) slab tin, 8 cm (3¼ inches) deep.

Remove the stalks from the silverbeet, kale or spinach and place in a heatproof bowl. Pour boiling water over the leaves, then leave to stand for 2 minutes before draining in a colander and leaving to cool. Place on paper towel and squeeze out any excess liquid. Cut into shreds about 8 mm (⅜ inch) thick.

Place the eggs, sweet potato and onion in a food processor and process until the sweet potato is finely chopped.

Transfer to a large bowl and using a large metal spoon, stir in the remaining ingredients, including the silverbeet, kale or spinach.

Pour into the tin, levelling out with a spoon.

Bake for 30–40 minutes, or until set.

Leave to stand in the tin for 10 minutes before cutting into squares to serve.

Ling, Green Tomato & Pesto Bake

SERVES 4

150 g (5½ oz) basil pesto

40 ml (1¼ fl oz) lime juice

400 g (14 oz) green tomatoes

400 g (14 oz) boneless,
skinless ling fillets, cut
into 4 cm (1½ inch) strips

60 g (2¼ oz) tasty cheddar
cheese, grated

While ling is specified for this dish, it is also delicious made with boarfish, flathead or blue grenadier fillets. The interaction between pesto, seafood and the acidity of lime is simply stunning. Green tomatoes bring texture to the dish. If it is not possible to purchase these, simply substitute with the least ripe tomatoes available.

The most delicious accompaniment is crusty bread, sliced and served alongside the bake.

~~~~~~~

Preheat the oven to 170°C (325°F). Grease an 18 x 28 cm (7 x 11¼ inch) baking dish, 5 cm (2 inches) deep.

In a bowl, stir the pesto and lime juice together, adding just a little water if necessary to make a spreadable consistency.

Cut the tomatoes into 8 mm (⅜ inch) slices.

Spread the base of the dish with half the pesto mixture. Top with half the tomato slices. Layer the fish strips on top to cover. Place the remaining tomato slices over this, then the remaining pesto mix and, finally, sprinkle with the grated cheese.

Bake for 20 minutes, or until the fish is cooked through. (You can test the fish with the tip of a sharp knife – if it flakes easily, then it is done.)

SERVES 6–8

1 egg yolk whisked with
  20 ml (½ fl oz) water,
  for glaze

FOR THE PASTRY

250 g (9 oz) plain (all-purpose) flour

½ teaspoon sea salt

½ teaspoon baking powder

125 g (4½ oz) cold salted butter

FOR THE FILLING

20 ml (½ fl oz) extra virgin
  olive oil

10 g (¼ oz) salted butter

½ teaspoon sea salt

½ teaspoon paprika

½ teaspoon dried thyme

½ teaspoon mustard powder

500 g (1 lb 2 oz) skinless chicken
  breast fillet

300 g (10½ oz) mushrooms,
  cut into 1 cm (½ inch) slices

1 small onion, diced

1 leek, white part only, cut
  into 8 mm (⅜ inch) slices

2 garlic cloves, crushed

1 teaspoon chopped thyme

300 ml (10½ fl oz) chicken stock

3 teaspoons cornflour
  (cornstarch) mixed to a paste
  with 30 ml (1 fl oz) cold water

125 ml (4 fl oz) pouring cream,
  whisked together with
  1 egg yolk

3 teaspoons lemon juice

sea salt, to taste

NOTE *The filling can be made
up to 2 days ahead and stored
in the fridge.*

214

Chicken Stroganoff Double-Crust Pie

In this warming winter dish, a luxurious creamy mushroom sauce blends with oven-baked chicken. Baking the chicken first seals in its juices and enhances the flavour.

~~~~~~~~

To make the pastry

Place the dry ingredients and butter in a food processor and process until the mixture resembles breadcrumbs. (Alternatively, this can be achieved by rubbing the ingredients together with your fingers.)

Transfer to a large bowl, make a well in the centre and drizzle in enough cold water – around 125 ml (4 fl oz) – to make a soft dough. Don't add more water than is necessary or it will become too wet. Wrap in plastic wrap and place in the fridge for at least 30 minutes to firm up before using.

To make the filling

Preheat the oven to 200°C (400°F). Heat the oil and butter in an 18 x 28 cm (7 x 11¼ inch) flameproof baking dish, 5 cm (2 inches) deep, for 5 minutes.

Meanwhile, combine the salt, paprika, thyme and mustard powder in a small bowl, then rub all over the chicken breast. Add the chicken to the hot dish and bake for 5 minutes, then turn and bake for 5 minutes more, or until just cooked through. Remove from the oven, cut the chicken into 1 cm (½ inch) pieces and set aside to cool.

Add the mushrooms, onion, leek, garlic and chopped thyme to the dish and stir to coat with the chicken juices. Heat over medium heat and sauté until the onion is soft, around 3 minutes. Stir in the chicken stock and bring to the boil. Thicken with the cornflour paste, boiling for 1 minute more. Remove from the heat and stir in the cream mixture and the lemon juice, then add the chicken pieces. Add sea salt, to taste, and set aside to cool.

To assemble for baking

Preheat the oven to 200°C (400°F). Grease a 20 cm (8 inch) round pie dish, 6 cm (2½ inches) deep.

Cut one-third from the pastry, cover and set aside. Roll the remaining pastry out on a lightly floured surface until large enough to fit the base and side of the dish. Press into place, spoon in the cool filling, then brush the upper pastry edge with a little cold water. Roll out the reserved pastry to make a circle large enough to cover the top. Lay the pastry top over the filling and crimp the edges together with your fingers or a fork to firmly seal. If desired, make small leaves from the scraps of pastry. Brush with the egg glaze. If using, place the pastry leaves on top and glaze. Prick the top in several places with a fork.

Bake for 10 minutes, then reduce the oven temperature to 170°C (325°F) and bake for 20–25 minutes more, or until the pastry is golden and the filling is piping hot.

Stout Cottage Pie

SERVES 6–8

FOR THE FILLING

3 teaspoons extra virgin olive oil

10 g (¼ oz) salted butter, plus 40 g (1½ oz) extra, melted

500 g (1 lb 2 oz) blade or chuck steak, cut into 1 cm (½ inch) cubes

600 g (1 lb 5 oz) beef mince

300 g (10½ oz) finely diced onion

3 garlic cloves, crushed

1 leek, white part only, finely sliced (optional)

3 teaspoons tomato paste (concentrated purée)

1½ tablespoons chopped sage

2 teaspoons tomato chutney

2 teaspoons barbecue sauce

2 teaspoons worcestershire sauce

½ teaspoon sea salt

375 ml (13 fl oz) stout

3 teaspoons cornflour (cornstarch) mixed to a paste with 40 ml (1¼ fl oz) cold water

FOR THE TOPPING

800 g (1 lb 12 oz) potatoes

50 g (1¾ oz) softened salted butter, diced

30 g (1 oz) sour cream or softened cream cheese

½ teaspoon sea salt, or to taste

140 ml (4½ fl oz) milk

In this homely, comforting pie a rich, stout-infused beef filling is topped with creamy mashed potatoes and finished with a golden butter seal. The richness of the beef is complemented with the dusky tones of fresh sage.

To make the filling

Preheat the oven to 160°C (315°F).

Heat the oil and the butter in a large, heavy-based saucepan over medium–high heat and sauté the diced beef for 5–8 minutes, or until well coloured. Add the mince and sauté for 10 minutes, or until it changes colour. Add the onion, garlic, leek (if using) and tomato paste and cook for 2 minutes more. Add the sage and cook for a few seconds longer. Stir in the chutney, sauces, salt, stout and 150 ml (5 fl oz) water.

Bring to the boil, stirring. Remove from the heat and transfer to a 20–23 cm (8–9 inch) square baking dish, 10 cm (4 inches) deep. Cover with foil and bake for 2 hours, or until the meat is tender. (Check during the cooking time in case the liquid is getting low. If it is, replenish with a little boiling water to just cover the meat.)

To make the topping

Meanwhile, peel the potatoes and cut into 4 cm (1½ inch) pieces. Place in a large saucepan and barely cover with cold water. Bring to the boil over medium–high heat, then reduce the heat to low and cook until the potato is very tender. Drain well. Mash with a potato masher.

Whisk the diced butter, sour cream or cream cheese, salt and half the milk to a creamy consistency, adding enough remaining milk (and perhaps even a little more) to make a creamy mash.

To assemble for final baking

Once the filling is cooked, remove from the oven and immediately stir in enough cornflour paste to thicken. Increase the oven temperature to 210°C (410°F).

Using a large metal spoon, carefully place the warm potato mash on the beef mixture. Spread the top out evenly with the back of the spoon, then drizzle with the extra melted butter. With the tines of a fork, make a decorative pattern on top.

Bake for 20–30 minutes, or until the topping is golden brown and crisp.

Leave to stand for 5 minutes before serving.

Pizza Pumpkins

SERVES 4–8

40 ml (1¼ fl oz) extra virgin
   olive oil

4 pumpkins (squash),
   around 500 g (1 lb 2 oz) each

250 g (9 oz) cherry tomatoes

FOR THE FILLING

250 g (9 oz) beef mince

250 g (9 oz) sausage mince

1 large onion, grated or
   very finely diced

2 garlic cloves, crushed

1 tablespoon chopped herbs
   (such as rosemary, oregano or
   basil) or ¼ teaspoon dried herbs

3 teaspoons tomato chutney

3 teaspoons worcestershire sauce

40 g (1½ oz) tomato paste
   (concentrated purée)

½ teaspoon sea salt

60 g (2¼ oz) salami or
   pepperoni, diced

60 g (2¼ oz) ham or
   rindless bacon, diced

40 g (1½ oz) red, green or yellow
   capsicum (pepper), finely diced

30 g (1 oz) kalamata olives, sliced

40 g (1½ oz) mushrooms, diced

30 g (1 oz) tasty cheese, grated

20 g (¾ oz) parmesan,
   finely grated

80 g (2¾ oz) fresh breadcrumbs

FOR THE TOPPING

40 g (1½ oz) tasty cheese, grated

20 g (¾ oz) parmesan,
   finely grated

In this substantial dish the pumpkins are scooped out and filled with a meat mixture containing all the elements of pizza. The pumpkin flesh takes on the beautiful flavours of the filling. The additions can be as varied as with a regular pizza – this recipe can be customised to suit all diners.

It has been my experience that pumpkin is a vegetable less than enthusiastically received on the plate of many people young and older. This dish has the capacity to turn this around – but even if it doesn't persuade ardent pumpkin-avoiders to eat the actual flesh, its nutritional goodness will have been infused into the filling.

To make the filling

In a large bowl, use a large metal spoon to mix the filling ingredients together until very well combined, then set aside.

To make the topping

Simply mix the two ingredients together and set aside until needed.

To prepare the pumpkins

Preheat the oven to 170°C (325°F). Pour the olive oil into a 25 x 35 cm (10 x 14 inch) baking dish, 8 cm (3¼ inches) deep.

Cut a small slice from the base of each pumpkin so that they will sit flat, then cut a slice from the stalk end. Scoop out the seeds and pulp from the stalk end and discard, leaving 1 cm (½ inch) of pumpkin flesh inside.

Place the pumpkins in the dish.

Divide the filling into four and press it into the pumpkins quite firmly, ensuring there are no air pockets. Sprinkle on the cheese topping.

Bake for around 1¼ hours. If the topping starts to brown too much, cover the dish loosely with foil.

Remove from the oven, carefully spoon out any of the liquid fat that has accumulated around the pumpkins and discard.

To make the sauce

In a saucepan over medium heat, combine the sauce ingredients and stir until smooth. Bring to the boil, then reduce the heat and simmer for 3 minutes.

FOR THE SAUCE

40 g (1½ oz) tomato paste
(concentrated purée)

40 ml (1¼ fl oz) tomato sauce
(ketchup)

1 garlic clove, crushed

3 teaspoons worcestershire
sauce

¼ teaspoon sea salt,
or to taste

½ teaspoon soft brown sugar
or maple syrup

1 teaspoon vinegar (any sort)

400 g (14 oz) tin diced tomatoes

2 teaspoons cornflour
(cornstarch) mixed to
a paste with 30 ml (1 fl oz)
cold water (optional)

To assemble for final baking

Remove the sauce from the heat and spoon over and around
the pumpkins.

Place the cherry tomatoes around the pumpkins and return the dish
to the oven for another 20 minutes.

After 20 minutes test to see if the filling is cooked through. This can
be done by inserting a meat thermometer into the centre – the reading
should be at least 70°C (150°F).

Serve the pumpkins drizzled with the sauce.

If wishing to make 8 serves, cut the pumpkins in half at serving time.

NOTE *If there is more filling than the pumpkins can hold, simply roll
the left-over mixture into meatballs and place around the pumpkins
in the last 20 minutes of baking, turning once. These can be served
alongside the stuffed pumpkin, or refrigerated and used the next day
as a sandwich filling or snack.*

Summer Tomato Pie with Pesto Cream

SERVES 6–8

1 egg, separated, for glazing

FOR THE PASTRY

300 g (10½ oz) plain
  (all-purpose) flour

½ teaspoon sea salt

150 g (5½ oz) cold salted
  butter, diced

1 spring onion (scallion),
  roughly chopped

1 egg yolk, lightly whisked

FOR THE FILLING

850 g (1 lb 14 oz) tomatoes

2 teaspoons tomato paste
  (concentrated purée)

½ teaspoon white
  (granulated) sugar

1 teaspoon sea salt, or to taste

2 tablespoons finely
  snipped chives

2 tablespoons chopped
  basil leaves

40 g (1½ oz) cornflour
  (cornstarch)

FOR THE PESTO CREAM

60 g (2¼ oz) mayonnaise

70 g (2½ oz) natural or
  Greek-style yoghurt

125 g (4½ oz) basil pesto

2 teaspoons lemon
  or lime juice

sea salt and white pepper,
  to taste

Bright and bold, this delicious pie epitomises the warmth of summer produce. The tasty tomato filling is complemented both by the herb pastry and the tangy pesto cream.

To make the pastry

Place the flour, salt, butter and spring onion in a food processor and process until the mixture resembles breadcrumbs. (Alternatively, this can be achieved by rubbing the ingredients together with your fingers, although in this instance you will need to finely chop the spring onions.)

In a bowl, whisk together the egg yolk and 70 ml (2¼ fl oz) cold water.

Transfer the flour mixture to a large bowl then, using a metal spoon, fold in enough egg yolk mixture to make a soft dough.

Wrap in plastic wrap and place in the fridge for at least 30 minutes to firm up before using.

To prepare the filling

Peel the tomatoes by dipping them in boiling water for a few seconds, then plunging into very cold water for a few seconds more. The skins should slip off easily. Cut the tomatoes into 6–8 mm (¼–⅜ inch) slices, discarding the stalk ends.

Place the tomato in a bowl with the tomato paste, sugar, salt, chives, basil and cornflour. Stir gently with a metal spoon to combine, ensuring that there are no lumps of cornflour present.

Taste to check if extra salt is needed.

To assemble for baking

Preheat the oven to 200°C (400°F). Grease a 20 cm (8 inch) round fluted flan tin with a removable base, 8 cm (3¼ inches) deep.

Cut one-third from the pastry, cover and set aside. Roll the remaining pastry out on a lightly floured surface until large enough to line the base and side of the flan tin with just a small overhang. Press it into place.

Whisk the egg yolk for the glaze and brush it over the pastry. Leave to dry for 2 minutes, then tip the remaining egg yolk into the egg white, whisk together, then brush the pastry once more. Leave to stand for 3 minutes. This double glazing is to ensure a good seal so that the tomato juices don't ooze through and make the pastry soggy.

Roll out the reserved pastry to make a pie lid. Spoon the filling into the pastry case and top with the pie lid. Crimp the edges together with your fingers or a fork to firmly seal. If desired, make small leaves from the scraps of pastry.

Whisk 2 teaspoons cold water with the remainder of the egg glaze to thin it down a little, then brush on the top of the pie. If using, place the pastry leaves on top and glaze.

Prick the top of the pie in six places with the tip of a sharp knife.

Bake for 15 minutes, then reduce the oven temperature to 170°C (325°F) and bake for 45 minutes more, or until golden brown.

Remove from the oven and leave to cool on a wire rack for at least 1 hour.

To make the pesto cream

In a small bowl, whisk together the mayonnaise, yoghurt, pesto and lemon or lime juice until well combined. Add salt and white pepper, to taste.

Serve slices of the pie with the pesto cream alongside.

Summer Tomato Pie with Pesto Cream
(recipe on pages 220–1)

Gluten-Free Sweet Potato Lasagne
(recipe on pages 224–5)

Gluten-Free Sweet Potato Lasagne

SERVES 8

1.8 kg (4 lb) sweet potatoes

300 g (10½ oz) tasty cheddar
  cheese, grated

60 g (2¼ oz) parmesan,
  finely grated

FOR THE MEAT SAUCE

20 ml (½ fl oz) extra virgin olive oil

1 kg (2 lb 3 oz) beef mince

250 g (9 oz) rindless bacon, diced

300 g (10½ oz) diced onion

150 g (5½ oz) mushrooms, diced

4 garlic cloves, crushed

120 g (4¼ oz) tomato paste
  (concentrated purée)

1 teaspoon dried oregano

3 teaspoons tomato chutney

3 teaspoons sweet chilli sauce

3 teaspoons worcestershire sauce

400 g (14 oz) tin diced tomatoes

½ teaspoon sea salt

3 teaspoons cornflour (cornstarch)
  mixed to a paste with 30 ml
  (1 fl oz) cold water (optional)

FOR THE CHEESE SAUCE

25 g (1 oz) cornflour (cornstarch)

600 ml (21 fl oz) milk

2 eggs, lightly whisked

90 g (3¼ oz) tasty cheddar
  cheese, grated

40 g (1½ oz) parmesan,
  finely grated

1 teaspoon dijon mustard

2 spring onions (scallions),
  finely chopped

½ teaspoon sea salt, or to taste

In this delicious version of lasagne, the creaminess of the sweet potato melds beautifully with the robust meat sauce and is complemented with a spring onion cheese sauce. This recipe is ideal for those who are gluten intolerant; I use maize cornflour instead of wheat-based, as well as gluten-free bacon.

Oven-roast or microwave the sweet potatoes until they are just tender. Leave to cool slightly, then remove the skin and cut the flesh into 3 mm (⅛ inch) slices. Set aside.

To make the meat sauce

Heat the oil in a heavy-based saucepan over medium–high heat and sauté the mince and bacon until well coloured, around 10 minutes. Add the diced onion and mushroom and cook for 5 minutes, then add the garlic and tomato paste and cook for 1 more minute.

Stir in the dried oregano, tomato chutney, sweet chilli sauce, worcestershire sauce, diced tomatoes and salt.

Bring to the boil, then reduce the heat and simmer uncovered for 20 minutes.

Gradually stir in enough of the cornflour paste to reach a thick consistency, then remove from the heat.

To make the cheese sauce

In a small heatproof bowl, whisk together the cornflour and 100 ml (3½ fl oz) of the milk. Add the eggs and whisk again briefly.

Heat the remaining milk in a saucepan over medium–low heat. When the milk has almost reached boiling point, pour 120 ml (4 fl oz) of the hot milk into the egg mixture and whisk. Now pour all the whisked egg mixture back into the saucepan of hot milk. Lower the heat and whisk until the mixture thickens, then stir in the tasty cheese, parmesan, mustard, spring onion and salt, to taste. Remove from the heat.

To assemble

Preheat the oven to 170°C (325°F). Grease a 25 x 32 cm (10 x 12¾ inch) baking dish, 8 cm (3¼ inches) deep.

Spread a thin layer of the meat sauce over the base of the dish and top with one-third of the sweet potato slices.

Spread with half the remaining meat sauce and then sprinkle 70 g (2½ oz) of grated tasty cheese on top.

Top with another third of the sweet potato slices, the last of the meat sauce and another sprinkling of tasty cheese.

Top with the last of the sweet potato slices, then spoon the cheese sauce on top.

Sprinkle the remaining tasty cheese and the parmesan over the cheese sauce.

Bake for 30 minutes, or until heated through and the cheese is bubbling and golden brown.

Leave to stand for at least 20 minutes before cutting into generous squares to serve.

Fennel & Onion Tart

SERVES 6–8

1 egg white, whisked

FOR THE EASY FLAKY PASTRY

250 g (9 oz) plain (all-purpose) flour

½ teaspoon baking powder

¼ teaspoon sea salt

180 g (6½ oz) cold salted butter, cut into 1.5 cm (⅝ inch) cubes

1 teaspoon lemon juice

1 egg yolk

120 ml (4 fl oz) ice-cold water

FOR THE FILLING

40 g (1½ oz) salted butter

40 ml (1¼ fl oz) extra virgin olive oil

250 g (9 oz) finely sliced fennel

250 g (9 oz) finely sliced onion

4 eggs

300 g (10½ oz) sour cream

40 ml (1¼ fl oz) dry white wine

1 teaspoon dijon or wholegrain mustard

2 teaspoons mayonnaise

2 teaspoons worcestershire sauce

1 teaspoon sea salt

2 tablespoons chopped thyme or ½ teaspoon dried thyme

FOR THE TOPPING

150 g (5½ oz) rindless bacon, diced

NOTE *If you haven't made flaky pastry before, this never-fail version is easy and the results are stunning. However, ready-rolled puff pastry can be substituted.*

Flaky pastry forms the basis for this deep-dish flan. The fennel and onion are sweated, not caramelised, and retain a gentle sweetness that is matched with a creamy thyme-infused egg custard.

To make the easy flaky pastry

Place the dry ingredients and butter in a food processor. Pulse for 2 seconds. Turn the machine off. Mix the ingredients around with a knife just a little, then pulse for 3 seconds more. Transfer to a large bowl.

In a small bowl, whisk together the lemon juice, egg yolk and ice-cold water until well combined. Gently stir almost all of this liquid into the dry mixture with a knife, reserving some of the liquid. The dough needs to come together quite easily. Do not over-mix – there should still be pea-sized lumps of butter evident.

Turn the dough out onto a lightly floured surface and pull together into a rectangle. Sprinkle lightly with flour and roll out to a rectangle 8 x 16 cm (3¼ x 6¼ inches). Fold the bottom third up to the middle, then the top third down over that. Turn the pastry 90 degrees, then roll out to the same size rectangle once more. Repeat this process three more times. Wrap in plastic wrap and place in the fridge for at least 30 minutes to firm up before using.

To make the filling

Heat the butter and oil together in a heavy-based frying pan over medium heat. Add the fennel and onion and gently sauté for 10 minutes, or until soft. Remove from the heat and allow to cool.

Meanwhile, in a bowl, whisk together the eggs, sour cream, white wine, mustard, mayonnaise, worcestershire sauce and salt until well combined and smooth. Stir in the thyme.

To assemble for baking

Preheat the oven to 210°C (410°F). Grease a 20 cm (8 inch) round flan tin with a removable base, 8 cm (3¼ inches) deep.

On a lightly floured surface, roll out the pastry until large enough to fit the base and side of the tin, with a slight amount of overhang. Press evenly into the tin and brush well with the whisked egg white to seal. Sprinkle the fennel and onion over the pastry case, then carefully pour the egg mixture on top and very gently stir to combine. Sprinkle the diced bacon over the top. Bake for 10 minutes, then reduce the oven temperature to 150°C (300°F) and bake for 40 minutes more, or until the filling is just set.

Leave to stand in the tin for around 20 minutes, or until cooled to lukewarm, before removing and cutting into wedges to serve.

Three Cheese & Spinach Rice Bake

SERVES 6–8

240 g (8½ oz) medium or long grain rice, or use left-over cooked rice (see Note)

4 eggs, lightly whisked

1½ teaspoons sea salt

300 g (10½ oz) coarsely grated onion

2 spring onions (scallions), finely chopped

¼ teaspoon dried thyme

¼ teaspoon dried oregano

2 teaspoons chopped thyme

2 teaspoons chopped oregano

3 teaspoons chopped flat-leaf parsley

100 g (3½ oz) tasty cheese, grated

60 g (2¼ oz) parmesan, finely grated

80 g (2¾ oz) feta, crumbled

2 teaspoons barbecue sauce

1 teaspoon worcestershire sauce

170 g (6 oz) finely shredded spinach leaves

300 ml (10½ fl oz) milk

150 g (5½ oz) rindless bacon, diced

40 g (1½ oz) salted butter, melted

This bake is filled with the goodness of spinach and garden herbs intermingled with three different cheeses and rice. Its crowning glory is its topping – a generous amount of bacon and butter – which completes the dish on a slightly decadent note.

Silverbeet (Swiss chard) can be substituted for the spinach, or even kale. The latter, however, should be steamed for 3 minutes before including, as some varieties take longer to soften during cooking.

Cook the rice, drain well and set aside to cool completely. (Doing this the day before you wish to serve is good but not absolutely necessary.)

Once the rice is ready, preheat the oven to 170°C (325°F). Grease an 18 x 28 cm (7 x 11¼ inch) baking dish, 8 cm (3¼ inches) deep.

In a large bowl, use a spoon to mix the eggs, salt, onion, spring onion, herbs, cheeses, sauces, spinach, milk and rice until well combined.

Transfer to the dish.

Sprinkle the bacon over the top, then drizzle on the butter.

Bake for 35 minutes, or until set.

Leave to stand for 10 minutes before serving.

NOTE *This recipe is a good way to use up any left-over rice. You will need about 800 g (1 lb 12 oz) cooked rice for this recipe. In fact, I often cook extra rice at another meal so that I can make this dish the next day. Be sure to cool and store cooked rice properly to avoid contamination.*

Acknowledgements

This book was truly a combined effort on the part of what came to be known as *The Comfort Bake* Team.

Spearheading the project at Murdoch Books was publisher Jane Morrow, who from the very outset so very well understood the concept of comfort baking and all that it encapsulates.

Others there included Virginia Birch (Editorial Manager), Megan Pigott (Design Manager), Martine Lleonart (Editor), Breanna Blundell (Editorial and Design Assistant) and Trisha Garner (Designer and Illustrator). I could not speak highly enough about their enthusiasm, professionalism, assistance and teamwork in bringing this book to fruition.

Any obstacle presented by an unforeseen circumstance at the beginning of the photo shoot was quickly overcome by the dedicated effort and unwavering support of Michael Smith, who stepped into the breach at little more than a minute's notice, baking the recipes in the book like the trooper and true friend that he is.

Cassie Lorraine was a wonderful asset in the kitchen, assisting and baking so capably as part of the team. As a fully qualified beautician, she was also the makeup artist for the photo shoot.

Granddaughter Charly Wood was kitchen hand for a day, proving that tender age is no hindrance to capability in the kitchen.

Food stylist extraordinaire Michelle Crawford made the bakes look their best and fit the mood of the book. Samuel Shelley worked alongside her, capturing the ethos of comfort baking with his excellent and meaningful photography.

Not to be forgotten are all my willing taste-testers. No one who came through our door could escape being conscripted to this role. In this respect, special mention should be given to the wonderful Custard Club (see page 68), the Wednesday morning tea group whose enthusiasm for my baking, and their sense of fun, provided huge inspiration for this book.

There were others too, who called in to visit and happily took up the task of taste-testing: family members, our friend of decades David Petrovic, neighbours, friends, acquaintances and, on occasion, grocery delivery drivers. No one was exempt.

It would be most remiss of me not to mention my husband, Robert, who – although he does not like to cook (other than the occasional poached egg) – toiled each of the nine days of the photo shoot, tending to the wood heaters to keep the three work areas warm on the frosty mornings. He also dedicated months of his time to sampling every single dish as it was baked during recipe development.

Thanks should also go to Chris Wisbey, whose wonderful morello cherries are pictured in the tart on the front cover. They were a gift from his extensive cherry orchards in the Coal River Valley. He has – since the very start – been unfailingly supportive and enthusiastic about my cookbooks.

Special mention must be made of the idyllic venue so generously provided to us on the final day of the photo shoot – Explorers Lodge. It is a delightful B&B situated close to the banks of the Derwent River here in our Valley.

Finally, and indeed very importantly, it is good to remember the ancient and accurate adage that we stand upon the shoulders of those who came before us. In this respect, my passion for all things baking came from the exceptional talent of two people in particular – my paternal grandmother and my very special Auntie Velma, my father's sister.

INDEX

Published in 2022 by Murdoch Books,
an imprint of Allen & Unwin

Murdoch Books Australia
83 Alexander Street
Crows Nest NSW 2065

+61 (0)2 8425 0100
murdochbooks.com.au
info@murdochbooks.com.au

Murdoch Books UK
Ormond House
26–27 Boswell Street
London WC1N 3JZ

+44 (0) 20 8785 5995
murdochbooks.co.uk
info@murdochbooks.co.uk

*We acknowledge that we meet
and work on the traditional lands
of the Cammeraygal people of the
Eora Nation and pay our respects to
their elders past, present and future.*

For corporate orders and custom publishing,
contact our business development team at
salesenquiries@murdochbooks.com.au

Publisher: Jane Morrow
Editorial Manager: Virginia Birch
Design Manager: Megan Pigott
Design and illustrations: Trisha Garner
Editor: Martine Lleonart
Photographer: Samuel Shelley
Stylist: Michelle Crawford
Home Economist: Cassie Lorraine
Production Director: Lou Playfair

Text © Sally Wise 2022
The moral right of the
author has been asserted.
Design © Murdoch Books 2022
Photography © Samuel Shelley 2022

Front cover photograph:
Cherry Tart, page 127.
Back cover photograph: Strawberry
Shortcake, page 58–60.

ISBN 978 1 92235 193 7 Australia
ISBN 978 1 91166 846 6 UK

NATIONAL
LIBRARY
OF AUSTRALIA

A catalogue record for
this book is available from the
National Library of Australia

A catalogue record for
this book is available from
the British Library

Colour reproduction by
Splitting Image Colour Studio
Pty Ltd, Clayton, Victoria

Printed by C&C Offset
Printing Co. Ltd., China

OVEN GUIDE: Cooking times will vary
depending on your oven. All recipes in
this book were tested in a fan-forced
oven; if using a conventional oven, set
the oven temperature 20°C (70°F) higher
than indicated in the recipe.

IMPORTANT: Those who might be at risk
from the effects of salmonella poisoning
(the elderly, pregnant women, young
children and those suffering from
immune deficiency diseases) should
consult their doctor with any concer[n]
about eating raw e[ggs.]

TABLESPOON MEASURES: We have [used]
20 ml (4 teaspoon) tablespoon meas[ures.]
If you are using a 15 ml (3 teasp[oon)]
tablespoon, add an extra teaspoon [of the]
ingredient for each tablespoon sp[ecified.]

10 9 8 7 6 5 4